MW01251685

ENCOUNTER *With* PURPOSE

A DIVINE APPOINTMENT WITH YOUR DESTINY

To Mrs. Dia
Much Love,
Nestor & Di—

By

NESTOR LIMA

ENCOUNTER WITH PURPOSE

Copyright © 2010 by Nestor Lima. All rights reserved.

No part of this publication may be copied, reproduced, or altered, partially or completely, or archived, nor transmitted using electronic, mechanical or other systems without the prior permission of the author, except for brief quotations.

Unless otherwise indicated, all Scripture quotations are taken from the Holy Bible, New International Version®. Copyright © 1973, 1978, 1984 International Bible Society. Used by permission of Zondervan Publishing House. All rights reserved.

Diligence has been made to source information as accurately as possible. Should you find an error in attribution, please contact the author.

www.NestorLima.com

Published by Nestor Lima Ministries
P.O. Box 2007
Hurst, TX 76053

ISBN: 1-4537250-0-8
Printed in the United States of America

Cover design by Miracle Media and Elizabeth Jaring
Cover photo: istockphoto / Toltek

DEDICATION

To my Lord and Savior:

Thank you for creating me fearfully and wonderfully. I fully embrace your divine design for me!

To my lovely bride:

For being a wonderful friend, a faithful companion, and a loving wife. Dina, thank you for your unconditional love and support!

To my purposeful daughters:

For your support and understanding throughout this project. Gianna, you have inspired me by publishing your first book when you were only 8-years old. Nathalia, thank you for the love and joy you share with me constantly, keep it coming!

ACKNOWLEDGEMENTS

Great goals are always achieved with the help of great people. This book is not an exception. I am thankful for all who have helped me to complete this book.

Several dear individuals contributed in different levels. Thank you for those who edited, reviewed, provided feedback and made suggestions and corrections, including the following fabulous people:

Dr. Iris Delgado, thank you for committing to go over the manuscript while ministering around the world.

Dr. Margarita C. Treviño, your critique of the content was invaluable.

Pastor Bill Earley, thank you for dedicating time out of your very busy schedule to read the manuscript.

Beverly Pettiway, a heart-felt thanks for proofreading the first draft of the manuscript.

Mr. Paul Nyamweya, I treasure your friendship. A million thanks for proofing the final copy of the manuscript!

Dina Lima, my precious bride, thank you for working on the manuscript countless hours and for encouraging me always!

Thank you all for your friendship and your contribution!

TABLE OF CONTENTS

FOREWORD

In this book, Nestor Lima helps the reader explicitly and amazingly to discover his or her life purpose.

In his work, he employs the existential bases, providing guidance and answers about the primary concerns of every human being, connecting the reader with the purposes for human life from God's creation.

His approach has two basic sources: one, his great experience as a Professional Certified Coach in the development of the potential, skills and abilities of people to achieve a meaningful life; the other, his wide perception and knowledge of the relevant biblical approaches to overall personal growth. Together, these sources combine to feed the need of every person to find the whys and wherefores of their existence, in the book of personal history that we call life.

It addresses the six dominant philosophies relevant to life and human purpose, and then compares these philosophies with the misconceptions that people usually have with these topics. Finally, the reader will be guided with precision, insight and sensitivity to take the steps that guides one not only to discover life's purpose, but also to live it out daily and with practicality.

Now dear reader, you should know something more about the author of this work. Nestor Lima has been a deacon, evangelist and teacher for over sixteen years. In the past eight years, his ministerial participation has developed in Anglo American churches in the United States of America. His activity has been associated with providing specialized conferences for marriage and family, for youth and singles, leadership, expertise and all matters related to life's purpose. As you will be able to appreciate, in this book we have found and will deal with an author who is highly effective, with extensive experience and outstanding vision. Therefore, we don't doubt the benefits that you can get by reading this book.

As if that were not enough, Nestor and his wife obtained doctorates in theology, respectively, an essential field of all ministry tasks, ecclesial and spiritual assistance. In addition, after three years of studies, Nestor received his Professional Certification as Coach (Professional Certified Coach) from the International Coach Academy.

One of Nestor Lima's sayings or expressions, most famous and influential, which has affected people who have thrived under his influence and teaching, is, "Your life purpose is the key that unlocks God's glory and greatness inside you." This powerful statement has the same meaning and direction of his philosophy of ministry, which refers to, "inspiring and empowering individuals to discover their life purpose." Extraordinary, isn't it?

In summary, the book *Encounter With Purpose* will not only leave a deep impression on its readers, but will produce vital shifts in terms of attitude, decisions and actions that will affect the product and end result of each person entering into fellowship with its pages. Furthermore, this book will not stay in the shelves of your personal library — it will pass from hand to hand, thereby increasing the transforming capacity of the ideas proposed by the inspired author.

In my capacity as a scholar of different subjects and disciplines and as a researcher in the fields of theology and humanities, I am sure that like me, dear reader, you will appreciate and take advantage of this reading.

Dr. René Peñalba
Author and international conference speaker
President and Founder of International Christian Center
Tegucigalpa, Honduras

PREFACE

I believe in uniqueness.

Every single human being is born with individual greatness. There is a specific reason why each of us is born. A task has been assigned for each of us to accomplish during the *days ordained* for us. The days ordained for *you* are different from those ordained for *me*.

When God created you, He didn't use a mold—and if He did, He used it once and then broke it! No one has ever, nor will ever, have your identical fingerprints.

Having gained greater awareness about our uniqueness, I became sincerely interested in discovering the reason for my existence. Similar to other people's experience, I embarked on this quest during a time that I faced a loss. It was during this season in my life that a thirst for digging deeper about my purpose was born. It became an insatiable passion. Today, I thank God for that "loss" that led me to a personal encounter with my purpose.

I resolved in my heart not to rest until my answer was revealed. I made a commitment and was fully determined that I would no longer live without *knowing* my purpose. Existing was not enough for me any longer. I was seeking to experience life at a deeper level. It was an intense time of praying, searching, reading, learning and reflecting. Everything I invested in this endeavor paid off. I discovered it! The more I meditated on it, researched it, and spoke about it to my wife, my daughters and friends, the clearer it became. As you read this book and discover the unique reason for your own existence, I make my individual contribution in this world and in God's ultimate plan. I discovered that purpose touches both the temporal and the eternal. This revolutionized my life!

My life purpose was further confirmed as I reflected on the notes of teachings and sermons I had shared during my first sixteen years as a Christian. Now I can see many clues about my purpose, even during the period of my life as a gangster! These manifested in different ways as I contributed to my peers by making them worse thugs, and often better soccer and basketball players.

During my quest, I began to connect the dots. Now I understand that purpose doesn't have to be a mystery. It can be revealed to us. We can know it. And once we do, we can live energized, focused, fulfilled and even more productive.

I pray that as you read this book, you too experience your own divine appointment.

May you have that unique encounter when purpose looks into your eyes and says to you, "Thank you for diligently seeking me! I have been waiting for you. Now, let's go make it happen!"

—Nestor Lima

INTRODUCTION

There are no two of you.

You and I are unique and original masterpieces. Whenever I turn on my laptop computer, I don't type in a password. Instead, I swipe my thumb on the digital fingerprint reader. This is possible in part to the technology available, but more importantly, because in more than 6 billion people currently living on planet Earth, no one else has the same fingerprint as I do. Thousands could line up and swipe their thumb on the reader of my laptop, but it wouldn't work for anyone else, just me. I love uniqueness!

The objective of this book is to provide inspiration, encouragement and guidance to discover your life purpose. As a result, you will become a more fulfilled and productive individual.

You will learn what is required and what to expect once you discover it. Different philosophical views will be explored, and common misconceptions will be unraveled. A sound foundation about the source and meaning of life's purpose will be established. Purpose will be considered from its eternal perspective, which will encourage you to see the big picture. You will be guided step by step to discover it. Lastly, you will find out how to transition and live your life purpose on a daily basis.

You may have had many questions about this topic. It is my desire that you find many answers in the proceeding pages of this book.

PURPOSE AND GREATNESS

I am delighted to coach you as you invest time reading this book. I have a passion and excitement about life, and it is my full intention to transmit that to you. Whenever I meet people, I see two things in them: purpose and greatness. You have been endowed with greatness. The solution to most of your problems and needs are tucked inside of you. My goal in life is to assist you to identify these great resources and to develop them to their maximum capacity.

I am confident that as you allow me to coach you through this book you will be enabled to identify your specific life purpose. You don't have to worry about not meeting my expectations or failing me as your coach. Failure is out of the picture. Embracing this reality moves you one step closer in your journey.

Why am I so confident about you? Why do I believe so much in you? Why is there no doubt in me that you can find your purpose? I am so glad that you are pondering these questions. The primary reason for my confidence is that I am not the one responsible for "assigning" your life purpose. Aren't you glad? If I were, you would probably love me or... love me even more!

The other reason for my confidence is that purpose has already been assigned to you. Purpose resides in you. The information contained in this book is designed to assist you in finding something you already possess.

My life purpose is to inspire and guide you to discover your life purpose, and to activate God's greatness that resides inside you. There is nothing that gives me greater satisfaction than to add value in these two areas of people's lives. I will assist you in discovering the purpose that has already been bestowed upon you. You have been designed on purpose and you have just embarked on a journey to discover it. Welcome!

ALIGNMENT

Whether it is a machine or our spine, they reach optimum performance when they are in alignment. To align ourselves with our Designer, we will approach the quest for purpose by paying special attention in the following three areas:

1. **INSIDE**

   Your personal design. This area focuses on you—your natural abilities, talents, inclinations, passions and dreams. You have been designed perfectly for your specific tasks on earth.

2. **OUTSIDE**

   Your life experiences. This area revolves around the things that life has prepared you for—beliefs, personal and spiritual experiences, wake-up calls and skills acquired through education and training.

3. **ABOVE**

   Your life purpose. This is determined, assigned and revealed by your Designer. You will not find it looking inside or outside; you must look above. Chapter 30 presents five different ways that life purpose is revealed.

Your life purpose should not be determined by considering only one of these aspects and disregarding the other two altogether. Most available secular discovery tools approach purpose with a temporal view of life. That is to say, they assist people to look inside and outside. With the information obtained, people are guided to formulate their life purpose. Such process leaves out one very important place: above.

In this journey, we will explore all three areas. In parts 1-5, the areas of your personal design and your life experiences will be addressed. Parts 6-7 will deal with life's purpose from a divine perspective.

Imagine for a moment how your life would be if you were in total alignment with your personal design, your life experiences and your life purpose. It is a possibility!

CREATED FOR GREATNESS

All of God's creation is blessed with greatness and uniqueness. Even the temporal forms of life such as plants and animals are saturated with beauty and glory. Human beings are superior to all other forms of creation. God placed humankind over and above everything else He created. We are endowed with beauty, glory, honor and greatness. And He deposited all that greatness inside us.

When the Psalmist David contemplated God's marvelous and vast creation, he also noticed the special place that God had assigned to humankind. David expressed his admiration and appreciation of God's work:

> When I consider your heavens, the work of your fingers, the moon and the stars, which you have set in place, what is man that you are mindful of him, the son of man that you care for him? You made him a little lower than the heavenly beings and *crowned him with glory and honor.* You made him ruler over the works of your hands; you put everything under his feet: all flocks and herds, and the beasts of the field, the birds of the air, and the fish of the sea, all that swim the paths of the seas. O LORD, our Lord, how majestic is your name in all the earth! (Psalm 8:3-9, emphasis added.)

The psalmist notices that the moon and the stars have been set in place to carry out their unique function. In the same manner, God has designed each one of us with a unique purpose. Once identified, or discovered, the greatness and *glory* God has placed inside us will start to manifest in its greatest form.

WILL THIS WORK FOR ME?

I enjoy sports and have the opportunity to coach young children in soccer. I love assisting them in developing their talents and abilities. Most of them, especially the ones under ten years of age, are unaware of the abilities they possess. One reason is that they don't "manifest" them to their maximum competence right away. Many get frustrated initially because they wish to see results immediately. Even though I am gifted to play soccer, I am not responsible for "granting" them the abilities and talents they need to become successful soccer players. However, it is my delight to help them tap into the resources that they are gifted with, and to coach them so they can develop their talents.

This is true in every sport and in life. I express my excitement to provide guidance as you journey in the quest to experience the power of living life on purpose.

You may think that this would work for somebody else, but it may not work for you. You may think you are too young or too old or in-between. The principles for discovering your unique purpose presented in this book will help you regardless of your age. Using these principles, my wife and I created an environment of purpose and personal growth in our home. As a result, our daughters discovered their purpose at ages four and six.

Every journey begins with one step. If this is your first step, welcome! Maybe you already have made a lot of progress in this journey, congratulations! Whatever your individual situation may be, I am delighted to walk beside you no matter where you are along this quest.

It is my firm belief that each person is designed for a specific purpose. Once discovered, it will invite you to embark on the most exhilarating ride of your life! Are you ready? Let's go make it happen!

ENCOUNTER WITH PURPOSE

PART 1

WHY
PURSUE PURPOSE

"The world makes way for the man who knows where he is going."

— Ralph Waldo Emerson

WHY PURSUE PURPOSE

Most of us, at some point or another, have asked ourselves the big question: What is my purpose in life? It is possible that you may not have verbalized it or shared it with someone else. However, this inquiry is *built-in*, per se. Most people have wondered, "What in the world was I created to be? What is the reason for my existence?" Some people wrestle internally with this matter. What you do when it surfaces in your mind is critical for the discovery of your purpose.

I believe this question ranks among the most important ones you will ever confront in life. It is a difficult issue to answer because it is very broad, and the possibilities seem to be endless. It strikes at the core of your being. It demands an answer that clearly defines who you are and explains the reason for your existence.

For the purpose of personally evaluating its depth, I suggest that at your earliest opportunity you drop this question to a couple of your friends or family members. Observe their physical reaction. Note carefully the first words uttered. Some people are shocked and don't know what to say. Others will say, "I have never been asked that before." I have seen some people squirm and immediately enter into a state of anguish as they unsuccessfully attempt to give a satisfactory answer. It is as if they are cornered against the ropes and their defense is down. Have fun with this experiment!

This part of the book will address the area of your personal design, which means that you will be looking *inside*.

Living on purpose will dramatically enhance your life in all aspects by gaining greater focus and direction. Ralph Waldo Emerson, a great American philosopher and poet, seems to have understood this concept when he said, "The world makes way for the man who knows where he is going."[1]

There are some exciting reasons for living on purpose. The following chapters will expose some of these reasons and the benefits you can experience when you discover your unique design.

CHAPTER 1

YOUR PURPOSE IS THE GREATEST EXPRESSION OF GOD'S GLORY

A life lived on purpose is the greatest expression of God's glory on earth!

You have been *crowned* with *glory* and *honor*. To be crowned means to be recognized officially with honor or recompense.[1] A synonym for glory is aura. Aura is a distinctive and intangible quality that surrounds a person. Honor is respect and esteem shown to someone.

When an athlete wins the race, honor is bestowed upon him by awarding him with a prize or trophy, and by officially recognizing and crowning him as the winner. In God's eyes, you are the athlete who has been crowned with glory and honor. When you discover and live out your unique purpose, the beauty and greatness of those trophies are revealed.

If you have never acknowledged verbally the fact that God has crowned you with glory and honor, I encourage you to do it at this moment and to start living with a heightened awareness of this awesome reality.

When you operate in the purpose for which you have been designed, you become the greatest expression of God's glory on Earth. Everything God created has glory. Just look at the plants with their wide variety of colors, shapes and smells. If you observe the animal kingdom, you can see the "glory" of each animal. It may be the majesty and strength of a lion; or the power of a horse; or even the camel's ability to travel about two weeks without water while carrying heavy loads through the desert.

Every creature in our world has its own unique design, beauty and elegance. When a bird flies, it manifests its unique glory; when a horse gallops with all its might, we witness its glory. The horse's glory cannot be seen when it is on water. And if we take a fish out of the water, its glory cannot be valued. All creatures have been designed to function in an environment that makes it possible for them to show off their unique *glory*. The horse doesn't soar and the eagle doesn't gallop, but each one is majestic in its unique design. Animals reveal their glory as they crow, fly, soar, swim, roar or gallop—as they do whatever it is they were created to do.

> *The glory of your uniqueness won't manifest in the greatest way possible unless you identify it first.*

You are unique. No one is better equipped to display your uniqueness than you are. Anyone attempting to be you is a phony, an imitation, and a counterfeit. The *glory* of your uniqueness won't manifest in the greatest way possible unless you *identify* it first. As you acknowledge it and start living with purpose, you align yourself with your Designer, the One who deposited greatness and glory inside you. As you live out your Designer's original intention, you roar with the confidence of the lion and soar to the heights of the eagle! Your contribution to this world becomes the greatest demonstration of the glory that God put inside you. You become great at what you do, enjoy it to the maximum, and experience the deepest contentment.

> *As you live with your Designer's original intention, you roar with the confidence of the lion and soar to the heights of the eagle!*

Your life purpose is the *key* that unlocks God's glory and greatness inside you.

CHAPTER 2

YOUR PURPOSE PROVIDES PERSONAL FULFILLMENT

Finding our life purpose is more important than we are told.

Most people don't realize that living on purpose provides the maximum satisfaction a human being could ever experience. In his book, *From Dream to Destiny*, Robert Morris, senior pastor of Gateway Church in Southlake, Texas, explains:

> Do you realize that you have the intellect, ability, talent and gifting to do something special for God? He designed you for a specific role—and you will never be truly happy until you discover what that role is. But when you discover your purpose and begin fulfilling it, your life will take on new energy and excitement.[1]

Very few other things in life can provide the depth of personal fulfillment and excitement, as when we live with purpose.

Aubrey Malphurs is an author and professor at the Dallas Theological Seminary. In his book, *Planting Growing Churches for the 21st*

Century, he writes, "We realize that there are some things we enjoy doing because we were designed to do them well."[2]

Unfortunately, some individuals don't attempt to discover their purpose because they are too busy with life and have not paused to take the time and effort it requires and deserves. For others, discovering their purpose seems so complicated and almost unachievable that they simply give up and decide to live life in what I call a "take whatever life gives you" mode. Thus, they live without planning or making goals for tomorrow, let alone next year. We all know that tomorrow is uncertain, but planning for it becomes very certain once you are operating in your purpose.

> *If you are not living on purpose, you are not living; you simply exist.*

These careless attitudes toward life are partially responsible for those that die on a daily basis without having fulfilled their purpose. I once heard someone say that the most expensive piece of real estate is not the Taj Mahal in India, nor is it found in downtown Manhattan. It's found in the cemeteries because buried there are unfulfilled dreams, unsung songs, unwritten books, and many other unrealized contributions to our world. This is a thought provoking observation, and it boils down to the tragedy of unfulfilled purpose.

Living on purpose requires focus and single-mindedness. The Bible explains the following:

> But when he asks, he must believe and not doubt, because he who doubts is like a wave of the sea, blown and tossed by the wind. That man should not think he will receive anything from the Lord; he is a double-minded man, unstable in all he does. (James 1:6-8)

Double-mindedness is the cause of broken focus — and lack of focus is the result of living life without a definite purpose.

I consider it a tragedy for people not to live out their life purpose. If you are not living on purpose, you are not living; you simply exist. George Bernard Shaw provokes us to recognize purpose as something great, "This is the true joy in life, the being used for a purpose recognized by yourself as a mighty one."[3]

THE TOP THREE REASONS THAT PROVOKE PEOPLE TO REFLECT ABOUT PURPOSE

The interviews I conducted during my research revealed the top three reasons that usually cause people to think about their life purpose.

1. LOSS

The surveys and interviews showed that the majority of people confront this question when they experience setbacks. It tends to happen when things are not going as planned and they have experienced a recent failure of some sort. It may be the loss of health, a loved one, a relationship, a job or a business. In a way, these "bad" experiences help to prepare us for an encounter with our purpose. You are probably thinking, "You mean to tell me that something good can come out of something bad?" Yes, that is correct! Napoleon Hill, author of *Think and Grow Rich*, encourages us to be optimistic about our setbacks because he believed that, "Every failure brings with it the seed of an equivalent advantage."[4]

Failure exists when we fail to learn from our failures. We all experience disappointments at one level or another, and we can learn many lessons from them.

2. DISSATISFACTION

Losses or setbacks can make us feel unfulfilled and unhappy with life. During these times, there is no spark in life and no love for living. The dissatisfaction may not necessarily have to do with lack of material things. It deals with much deeper issues like personal meaning and significance.

On the other hand, there are those who believe that satisfaction is found in material possessions. They wake up one day and realize they are now owned by their possessions. Education and affluence has given them a higher position within the standards of socio-economic circles. Yet if you listen to the daily news, you can clearly see that these advantages alone don't necessarily translate into happiness, contentment or fulfillment.

Others seek to cure this condition by going into a relationship, getting married, having children, achieving certain goals linked to a career, sports or the accumulation of other assets. The notion is that by fulfilling these goals, a permanent state of happiness will be secured. After the pride and glory of achieving these goals has worn out, the feeling of unhappiness returns. It is during these times that the question about life's purpose surfaces very frequently.

Dissatisfaction can lead us to feel unimportant and thus raise all kinds of questions about life, ourselves and the role we play in this world.

Often people will turn to any available means to discover their life purpose. I have found that there are plenty of different life purpose philosophies out there. Many of these schools of thought could get you even more confused.

3. AGE

As I share about this topic with people who are beyond their fifties, many of them are unable to contain their tears. They express frustration and desire to discover their purpose. I sense their pain and realize that life could be more meaningful for them. It may be disheartening for people who have struggled with this question for decades yet still not have a satisfactory answer. It can be difficult to consider the journey in life and still not have peace with such an important issue. If this is your situation, I will assist you to turn such feelings of frustration into energy and motivation that will enable you to identify your purpose.

One of my coaching clients was a 72-year-old woman. After a few sessions, she called me to inform me that she had gotten her spark back. She said that it was as if dynamite had been ignited inside her and she was so happy!

WAKE-UP CALLS

Dewayne Owens, author of the book *How to Get Rich On Purpose*, likens some situations we experience in life to "wake-up" calls. It seems as though things that come our way are purposeful. If we can discern them, we will be able to see that somehow they are saturated with clues and provide guidance toward our purpose. Here is how Dewayne explains this:

> Purpose provides you the opportunity of receiving a wake-up call, which gives you a revelation that your life is meant to be more than it currently is. Wake-up calls will take the scales of blindness off of your eyes so that you can see the truth in your life … Wake-up calls are necessary because without them many of us would live out a meaningless existence … It is only one way to recognize a wake-up call. It is when an event or circumstance convinces you of a need to make a major change in your life … A wake-up call will normally hit you when life is not going well. It will alert you at your lowest moments of despair when hope seems slim. Our wake-up calls come at these hard times because we have ventured far off the path of purpose. We have taken such a detour from our purpose that it is absolutely necessary for us to receive a wake-up call to bring us out of the circumstances that we have created for ourselves.[5]

In the same book, Owens shares how he received his personal wake-up call and how he responded to it. He was addicted to marijuana and cocaine and was informed that his employer had decided to perform random drug tests. That was his wake-up call! He could choose to risk his livelihood or to create a major change in his life. Owens explains that this was one of the toughest things he had ever done, but he gave up the addiction. Eventually, he became a motivational speaker, author and trainer.

In their book, *The Power of Focus*, Jack Canfield, Marc Vincent Hansen and Les Hewitt express their genuine desire for people to start living their purpose now and not wake up one day when life has passed them by. They write:

> We don't want you to end up like masses of other people out there, wondering generalities that are unsure of what they are doing, and why they are doing it. Then there are those people who come to a cross-roads in their life. Somewhere between thirty-five and fifty-five years of age, the famous life crisis appears. Suddenly deeper questions begin to surface like, "is this all there is?" After some serious navel-gazing, they begin to feel a void, a sense of emptiness. Something is missing, but they can't quite put their finger on it. Gradually they come to the realization that just collecting material things and paying off the mortgage isn't doing it for them anymore.[6]

I consider that the greatest tragedy in life is to approach the end of our days without having made a significant contribution during the days ordained for us. Such contribution doesn't necessarily have to be big in numbers, but it must transcend temporal life.

You can avoid the tragedy of living life without purpose. The way to do it is not to become a tragedy but rather design a strategy.

CHAPTER 3

YOUR PURPOSE IS
YOUR COMPASS

Your purpose is your compass in life.

If you don't know where you're going, any vehicle will take you there. If you don't aim at anything, you will always hit your target.

It is hard to arrive at a place you have not yet defined. Traveling doesn't guarantee that you will arrive somewhere. If you haven't identified your destination and you decide to travel, how will you know when you get there? Bishop T.D. Jakes, senior pastor and founder of the Potter's House in Dallas, Texas, states the following about life's direction:

> Like our friends in the "Lost" series, we all lose our perspective when we do not have the navigation we need to find out where we are and what we need to fix the problems that have occurred.[1]

The means of transportation you choose is determined by your

destination. Imagine waking up one day and wanting to go somewhere, but you don't really know where. You walk to the nearest bus
stop or subway. You board the first vehicle that comes your way. The
fact that you don't know where it's going doesn't bother you a bit. In
fact, it doesn't even matter because you have no clear picture of your
desired destination anyway. Sadly, this scenario depicts the life of
many individuals around the world.

People who have not yet found their purpose live without a sense
of direction. They board *any vehicle* that comes their way. These
vehicles are merely distractions to steer them off the path that leads to
finding and fulfilling their true purpose. They come in many shapes
and forms. I consider the following some of these *vehicles*: unproduc-
tive habits, drugs, alcohol, immorality, pornography, marital infideli-
ty, profanity, and the like. Some of these often masquerade
themselves as meaningless hobbies that simply rob you of your most
precious commodity — time. People who live without knowing where
they are going in life are more likely to board such vehicles.

I am deeply saddened when I speak with individuals who are totally lost as to what they want to do in life. They have no clue how
they would like to contribute in this world. Individuals who live this
way lack the following:

- **Stability**: They are unstable in most areas of their lives.
- **Progress:** They seem to be in the same place as they were
  years ago. They don't make significant progress in their fin-
  ances or their personal and spiritual development.
- **Confidence**: They are more prone to avoid situations because
  they lack the self-assurance to confront them.
- **Direction:** They don't have a set course in life; they always
  follow. They become people pleasers.
- **Decisiveness**: Life is composed of a series of constant decisions. Since they don't know where they're going, decisions

become a dreaded task.

One night as I was coming back home from dropping off a friend, I suddenly found myself completely lost. Even though the place was only about fifteen minutes from my house, this was my first time in that neighborhood. I made one turn, came to a red light and had no idea which way to go. I became totally lost in my world for a moment. As I waited for the light, I was figuring out what to do. Suddenly I remembered that my car's rear view mirror has a built-in compass. One glance at the compass gave me the direction I needed desperately at that precise moment. I was in the same place, but I was no longer lost. With the direction obtained, I could make a sound decision. Instantly I knew I had to

> *People who don't know their life purpose are as a ship without a navigation system in the sea of life!*

go west to get back home. This was a small incident, and I could have used other methods to find my way home. However, not knowing where I was and where I needed to turn at that moment was one deeply disturbing experience for me. It produced an awful and helpless feeling. People who don't know their life purpose are as a ship without a navigation system in the sea of life!

John C. Maxwell is a top expert in leadership and personal development. Maxwell quotes the writer Catherine Anne Porter in reference to people's commitment to personal growth:

> I am terrified at the lack of objectives with which many live their lives. Fifty percent do not pay attention where there are going; forty percent are indecisive and they will go in any direction; only ten percent know what they want and not even all of them pursue it.[2]

One of the beauties of discovering and living life on purpose is that decisions become more meaningful. You develop a new way of making decisions. After you know where you're going, you start to take the proper steps and to make the adequate decisions to get you there. Knowing your purpose enhances your decision-making abilities as all your decisions become *purpose-conscious.* When direction is lacking, the results of decisions are not nearly as important, because one is not necessarily seeking a specific outcome. However, when we live on purpose, every decision matters greatly, because their results have a direct effect on the road we are pursuing.

When a vehicle invites you to get on board, your decision-making mechanism, which is your will, studies, analyzes and judges that vehicle. You arrive at a conclusion based on the following criteria:

- Where will this vehicle transport me concerning *my* purpose?
- Is it going to take me backward?
- Is it going to steer me off?
- Is it going to advance me toward my purpose?

Where are you going? We're all headed somewhere. Without the benefits of the compass — your life purpose — that somewhere may be … nowhere!

DECLARATION

World, open your doors to me because I know where I am going and my decisions are purpose-conscious!

CHAPTER 4

YOUR PURPOSE UNLOCKS
YOUR SUCCESS

True success cannot be experienced without knowing our life purpose.

John C. Maxwell quotes Henry J. Kaiser, founder of Kaiser Permanente, "There is overwhelming evidence that indicates that you cannot begin or achieve the best of you unless you have established an objective for your life."[1]

The best of you is released when you live your life on purpose. People who discover it often do better financially than those who set out just to make money. The reason is simple: We are better at doing our purpose than we are at doing anything else.

I love how Maxwell defines success: "Knowing your purpose in life, growing to reach your maximum potential and sowing seeds that benefit others."[2]

That covers a lot of ground. Once you discover it, the next step is to focus on growing and mastering the area of your life purpose. You become successful as you affect others. Maxwell explains this clearly:

> When we have a dream, we're not just spectators sitting back hoping that everything turns out all right. We're taking an active part in shaping the purpose and meaning of our lives. And the winds of change don't simply blow us here and there. Our dream, when pursued, is the most likely predictor of our future. That doesn't mean we have any guarantees, but it does increase our chances for success tremendously.[3]

The conveniences we enjoy, which have become so common to us, were invented, created or discovered by people who had a sense of purpose. They *knew* what they wanted. They could *see it* before creating it. They saw the value and understood that their contribution in life would fulfill needs of others, as they lived out their purpose.

Having a clear knowledge and understanding of your purpose is one of the main ingredients for experiencing success in life.

Referring to life's fundamentals, Les Hewitt provides the following counsel:

KNOW WHAT YOU WANT
KNOW WHY YOU WANT IT

DISCOVER YOUR TALENTS
USE THEM DAILY

WORK HARD
WORK SMART

GIVE UNCONDITIONALLY
LOVE UNCONDITIONALLY

FIND YOUR PURPOSE

LIVE YOUR PURPOSE[4]

A common thread that runs through all successful people is their unambiguous *knowledge* of what they want to accomplish in life.

CHAPTER 5

YOUR PURPOSE CLARIFIES
YOUR PAST

Purpose will answer many questions about your past.

Past experiences and interests serve as confirmation of your newly discovered purpose. As I look back at my own life, many questions have been answered with regard to my personality, things I have done, the way I have seen life, words I have spoken and teachings I have shared. Throughout my life, I can now see a trail filled with clues about my purpose. They are as dotted lines I would have been able to connect had I then been pursuing to know my purpose.

Chapter two of the book of Exodus documents the beginning of the story of Moses, the man God used to liberate the Israelites from slavery in Egypt. He is a great example of someone who is seeking answers for the specific way he or she handled certain situations in the past.

Even though Pharaoh's daughter had raised Moses, he knew that he was related to the Israelite slaves. One day, he noticed an Egyptian beating a defenseless Hebrew slave, who was most likely exhausted and unable to meet the labor requirements imposed upon him. Moses was filled with a sense of *need to defend* him. He took action. In fact, he killed the Egyptian and buried him in the sand, hoping no one had seen him.

The next day, Moses' crime was uncovered, and he fled for his life. He arrived in the land of Midian and rested by a well. Reuel, also known as Jethro, was the priest of this land, and he had seven daughters. While Moses rested by the well, Reuel's daughters came to draw water for their father's flock. Some shepherds also showed up and harassed these women. Again, Moses felt that same *need* to take action and *deliver* these disadvantaged women. He drove those shepherds away and assisted Jethro's daughters water their flock. Through this action, he also earned a wife.

Moses had *LIBERATOR* written all over his forehead since he was a child. His life purpose seeds were beginning to sprout. His actions were clues of his personal design. Many years later, he found himself *delivering,* setting free, not one individual nor a handful, but hundreds of thousands. He was the man for that task. He was born into the right family, in the right place, and at the right time.

Whenever Moses looked back at his life, he could see his past filled with clues about his purpose. During times of challenges, frustrations and questioning if he should continue leading the people through the dessert, his sense of purpose became the fuel that kept him going. I can picture Moses sitting in the back of a mountain reflecting and saying to himself, "My purpose explains the way I acted when I confronted certain situations in my past."

When you discover your life purpose, many things from your past will become clear. Additionally, you may uncover answers to such questions as to why you did what you did, and why things unfolded, the way did. With regard to this experience, Robert Morris explains:

> After you have stepped into your destiny, [purpose] you will look back, just as Joseph did (see Gen. 45:5-8), and understand the specifics of your purpose. You will say, "Oh, now I understand why I had to go through that. Now I know why God brought me here. This is the reason God worked in my life in that way. This is the reason things happened the way they did. Now I understand the purpose of all those things that happened!"[1]

What is the fuel that keeps you ticking? As you study your past, notice the actions you took during specific circumstances in your life. You may find your past filled with clues about your individual purpose!

PART 2

SEARCHING
WISELY

"So press on with the search. Strive to understand more about yourself and the role you were designed to play."

— Jack Canfield

SEARCHING WISELY

The first part presented five reasons for pursuing your life purpose. In this section, we will explore six great benefits you will experience when you indentify it. These will be like powerful fountains springing up inside you.

You will be acquainted with what is required of you to discover and identify your life purpose, so that you can apply yourself in the best way possible. When you compare all the benefits of living a life on purpose with the efforts required, you will realize that everything you put into this journey is well worth it.

Anything worthwhile in life requires some kind of effort. Fast food is convenient when you are on the go, but you cannot compare it to the quality of a home cooked meal! What is the difference? It will take you about five minutes to go through the drive-through and get your meal. However, preparing a home cooked meal will require much more time and effort on your part.

Many people know that they have a purpose, but not all of them know how to discover it. Others are simply unwilling to do what is necessary to discover it and live it out. When I was in technical school, one of my computer teachers used to say that you cannot get ten pounds of potatoes out of a five-pound bag. In life, we can only get out what we put in.

I have had clients apply themselves totally to this sacred journey, and as a result, they have properly identified their life purpose after a few sessions. I have shared the same information with others who have expressed a great desire to know their purpose, but their efforts have proved otherwise. Most of those that fully commit and dedicate themselves wholeheartedly experience the joy of discovering their life purpose, or at least gain greater clarity than ever before. On the other hand, the ones unwilling to put the necessary effort on their part only get out whatever they are willing to put in.

My desire is that you get the most as you embark on this journey to discover or reaffirm the reason for your existence.

CHAPTER 6

THE BENEFITS

Purpose provides multiple benefits.

When purpose is revealed, it will bring with it many additional advantages. These may come at you like a flood. Don't panic. It's okay! Following are six benefits you may experience in your own encounter with purpose.

1. INCREASED ENERGY

When you discover your life purpose, a surge of energy comes all over your body, and no matter how big the task, it becomes attainable. This energy or power is directly related to your life purpose. It resides inside all of us in a *standby* mode. It is waiting for its *own* channel to flow through. Your purpose *is* that channel. Your purpose unleashes that energy. You will be excited, and you won't need to hide it! This energy is the anointing on your life. It is a propelling force—the fuel that energizes you. It will keep you going when the going gets tough. It's what will keep you up until three or four o'clock in the morning studying, researching, learning, planning and strategizing. This energy released inside you will cause you to go places and to do things that you didn't dare to do before.

One day my family and I went to see a dog show. We were amazed and entertained with their abilities to leap and catch Frisbees. Before engaging the dogs with the Frisbees, the trainers educated the audience. The dogs couldn't wait. We could almost hear them say, "Throw me the Frisbee already!" The wait was torture for these performers. Their energy was coming out of their skin! The trainers did their best to hold their energy and enthusiasm. As soon as the leash came loose, off they went! Their energy was available because a "channel of distribution" was provided to them.

> *Uncertainty creates doubt; knowing your purpose creates confidence.*

Have you ever felt like you needed to do something with your life but you didn't know exactly what or through which channel? This ambiguous state doesn't provide the energy you need to do it, because you don't know what it is you want to do. If this energy was released in such a state, it would thrust you a thousand miles per hour in a thousand different directions. You would end up worse than Humpty Dumpty!

Don't torture the energy waiting within you. Provide the release it needs to manifest itself—namely, your life purpose!

2. INCREASED CONFIDENCE

You will walk with such confidence that impossibilities about fulfilling your purpose become so minute they just about disappear. It is not arrogance—it is poise. This assurance becomes evident to the people you deal with. This confidence is definitely not pride, although it can be interpreted as such. However, it is born out of *knowing* who you are and *where* you are going. Uncertainty creates doubt; knowing your purpose creates confidence.

Confidence is lacked when you are uncertain about what you are doing or where you are going. An inspirational quote from Stan Smith states, "Experience tells you what to do; confidence allows you to do it."[1]

> *Your purpose is your journey in life. When you discover it, you travel with confidence!*

Good instructions to get to a place give you a degree of assurance, but you never drive there with the same confidence as when you know *exactly* how to get there. Your purpose is your journey in life. When you discover it, you travel with confidence!

3. INCREASED FOCUS

Lack of focus can make one's life unfruitful. John C. Maxwell documents William H. Hinson's explanation as to why animal trainers carry a stool when they go into a cage of lions:

> They have their whips, of course, and their pistols are at their sides. But invariably they also carry a stool. Hinson says it is the most important tool of the trainer. He holds the stool by the back and thrusts the legs toward the face of the wild animal. Those who know maintain that the animal tries to focus on all four legs at once. In the attempt to focus on all four, a kind of paralysis overwhelms the animal, and it becomes tame, weak and disabled because its attention is fragmented.[2]

Obtaining a higher degree of focus doesn't mean you become immune to the challenges and adversities. However, you face them in a very different perspective.

Purpose not only includes what you do but it also excludes what you don't do. Once you know what you have been designed for, your purpose becomes your focal point. Focus is concentrated energy. The energy made available to you as a result of discovering your purpose now has a definite target. The results are astounding! A new realm of possibilities opens up before your eyes every single day.

4. INCREASED PERSONAL GROWTH

Don't be surprised if the personal growth you experience in the next twelve months after discovering your purpose is far greater than that of the last five to ten years! This is not something you will force. It will come naturally and it will surprise you. One reason for this rapid growth is the increased energy, confidence and focus that you experience. Jack Canfield explains it this way:

> When you are living on purpose, you feel that you are making a difference. And you don't need to be famous. You can make a significant impact in your own community. Another important factor as you explore your direction is your level of enthusiasm…You feel energized. When serving a purpose larger than yourself, your level of commitment also expands.[3]

When you discover your purpose, you will be operating in the *natural flow* of things. You will be in harmony with who you are, and focused on your desired accomplishments in life. You will excel in your area of focus instead of possibly going against it.

5. INCREASED DESIRE FOR MENTORS

The growth you experience will give you a desire to have mentors. The need for them will possibly become more evident than ever before. Mentors are those who teach us through relationships. They have knowledge we need. Their insight can prevent us from making costly mistakes. Their counsel helps us grow as they encourage, inspire, instruct and guide us.

A few months after I discovered my life purpose, I wrote letters to a couple of men whom I highly respect. I told them about my encounter with purpose and expressed my desire for them to be my mentors. I will share more about mentors in the final section.

6. INCREASED DIRECTION

This sense of direction alone causes you to view decisions in a completely new light. The awareness of your desired destination also brings a new perspective about the way you manage your time. Having a clear target gives you the direction you are seeking and causes you to recognize that there is a timeframe to achieve it.

> *Having a clear target of where you are heading gives you the direction you are seeking.*

Purpose unfolds the road map for life. Most people will not travel without first consulting their map or guide, especially when traveling by car. This information enables them to visit the best places and avoid the undesired ones. We invest time preparing for vacation trips and planning the things to do when we get there. Sadly, most people spend more time planning for a week's vacation than they do for their life. Jimmie L. Lucas Jr. writes:

> Did you know that the average person does not have goals in life? In reality, most people are walking around without any direction at all. Their lack of direction is evident by statements such as these: What am I going to do with my life? God, I need help! I just feel like giving up; it's not worth it...[4]

The most effective way to set goals is to create them based on your *values* and your life *purpose*. This means that your values need to be defined and your purpose discovered. It is then that you can set clear and worthy goals. Purpose becomes your standard for your plans and lifetime goals. Because of this awareness, you make sure that your plans and goals *line up* with your purpose. The closer your goals align with your values and your life purpose, the more likely you will achieve them. Your life purpose is what you align your goals with, thus providing you the *direction* you need in life.

My life purpose is to assist you in the discovery of your own purpose, and to empower you to activate the greatness that resides inside you. *That* is why I have written this book. It also explains why I am constantly applying myself in the areas of life's purpose, greatness in light of God's supreme plan, personal development and personal leadership. It gives me *direction*.

Your purpose is the billboard in life that points you in the right path. Your life purpose includes what you do, and it excludes everything you don't do. It points you in the way you should go and the paths you shouldn't follow. Robert Morris states it this way, "Your purpose provides *direction* toward your destiny, but it is important to understand that your purpose does not contain the *specifics* of your destiny."[5]

Your purpose is your compass for life. When you discover it, your life journey becomes an exciting expedition!

CHAPTER 7

WHAT IS REQUIRED
OF YOU

Purpose has priceless rewards.

As the term implies, a reward has certain requirements prior to its enjoyment. How long it takes to discover your purpose is highly determined by your pursuit. The evidence of desire is determination. In a way, this gives you a degree of control. How profound is your desire to have an encounter with purpose? How much do you desire for purpose to look into *your* eyes? I am not going to place a timetable for your discovery. In my experience, this varies with each person. There are many determining factors involved. Following are a few examples of how long it has taken some individuals to discover it.

Katie Brazelton, a women's Bible study director at Saddleback Church in South Orange County, says that in 1988 she started wondering if her purpose had something to do with nurturing seedlings. For many years, this vague idea kept flashing in her mind. Brazelton writes:

> It was not until 1994, six years after the ideas first began to form, that God made the vision clear. All along, He slowly had deposited in my soul distinct sensory images and impressions of His future plans for me. At last, it was time for Him to reveal the purpose that would hold my heart gratefully forever. Finally, I could identify the passionate ache in my heart. It was my life's purpose, the search for which had driven me crazy for years.[1]

The experience of one particular client I coached in her own discovery was different. After four weekly one-hour sessions, she e-mailed me to share her findings. She was so excited! Her life purpose became so obvious to her. She shared with me that the process was very easy to follow and didn't struggle or agonize over it.

I coached someone else for about 18 months. At times, she felt she had discovered it, but it didn't settle 100 percent with her. We kept working on it. Then one day, there it was! The discovery of her purpose had taken place. She was extremely happy! Her persistence was rewarded.

How long it takes to discover your purpose is highly determined by your pursuit.

So, how long will it take you to discover your life purpose? Although your experience will be individual, your passion will greatly influence its discovery.

Following is a list of factors to consider as you embark on this journey of self-discovery. Integrating these perspectives is highly recommended.

1. MAKE TIME

Finding one's purpose requires investing time and effort. I want to congratulate you for reading this book, which is a tool designed to assist you in finding what on earth you were created to do.

Time invested is not time wasted. Expect great results for your dedication. Purpose awaits you. You have started this wonderful journey, and now it is simply a matter of time before you make one of the greatest personal discoveries in your entire life!

2. BE DETERMINED

Discovering your purpose requires determination and a willing heart. You will need to decide to know more about yourself so you can be equipped to start living life in a dimension of true meaning and fulfillment. In their book, *The Power of Focus,* the writers speak about this required determination:

> Living your purpose requires single-mindedness — a resolve to do whatever it takes. It separates the weak from the strong, the procrastinators from the truly committed. It inflames a deep passion and creates a feeling of significance. When your purpose is clear, your life will have meaning. You will sleep at night fulfilled, instead of worrying about all the day-to-day stuff that creates stress and tension.[2]

It was a freezing cold Saturday morning. I had planned to attend a conference in which Bob Harrison was the main speaker. My wife had another commitment and had left home earlier. To my surprise, she had taken the set of keys to both of our cars and left the set that only had one key. Of course, the set she had left had the key to the car she was driving. The drive was only about ten minutes from our house to the conference location. It was before nine o'clock in the morning and I didn't want to bother anyone that early. I was determined to be there, so all I could think about at that moment was to start walking.

After fifteen minutes of trudging along in the cold weather, my face and ears were almost frozen. I called information and got the number to the church. I explained my ordeal to them. They were very helpful and arranged for someone to pick me up. I waited in the bitter cold for another fifteen minutes. It surely felt like it was a lot longer. I missed the first thirty minutes of that morning's conference session, but I was sure glad I made it!

Some door prizes were awarded during the second session. The person I had spoken with on the phone was the one leading the event. He shared about the situation I had gone through that morning and said that my determination needed to be rewarded. I received a CD and Bob Harrison's book entitled *Power Points for Success*. I was very happy! We should never forget that determination is always rewarded.

Are you determined? Do you possess the fortitude, resilience and stamina this journey may require? Your pursuit will be rewarded with the discovery of your purpose.

3. SEEK PURPOSE AS SOMETHING OF GREAT VALUE THAT YOU HAVE MISPLACED

When we misplace something of great value, we often use a process of sifting and sorting through things and places. If there is a pile of things, we start removing items from the top and work our way to the bottom. Most of the time what we are looking for is at the very bottom. I don't know why it works that way! Finding our life purpose may require a similar process.

In my search for my life purpose, I had to sift through a high pile. When I had removed one layer, I thought I would find it in the next — but it didn't happen. I kept on digging stuff out and removing layer after layer until the day came when there it was, looking straight into my still brown eyes. It was as if purpose was smiling at me and said, "Thank you for diligently seeking me! I have been waiting for you. Now let's go make it happen!"

I compare the discovery of purpose to that of onion peeling. With each layer removed, you get closer to the core. These layers exist in the form of wrong philosophies and misconceptions regarding the meaning of life and our purpose.

Purpose is not something you've lost; it's something you've not yet discovered.

Purpose is not something you've lost; it's something you've not yet discovered. It is a treasure awaiting you. Felix Adler provokes our thinking about this:

> The human race may be compared to a writer. At the outset, a writer has often only a vague general notion of the plan of his work, and of the thought he intends to elaborate. As he proceeds, penetrating his material, laboring to express himself fitly, he lays a firmer grasp on his thought; he finds himself. So the human race is writing its story, finding itself, discovering its own underlying purpose, revising, recasting a tale pathetic often, yet nonetheless sublime.[3]

Your discovery activates your purpose. It goes into motion the moment you tap into it. The benefits of life's purpose are reserved for the diligent seekers, not the casual observers.

4. SEARCH, LISTEN, LEARN

Discovering your purpose also requires an open mind and the willingness to search, to listen, and to learn. You will need to search your soul, listen and learn. It will be like an x-ray examination. Become a student of yourself. Make it a point to get to know you better. In fact, this quest is what personally escorted me to my purpose. I started studying and learning how my spirit, my soul (mind, emotions and will) and my body interact with each other. My goal was to learn to cooperate with God as He speaks into my spirit, instead of counteracting His voice.

Our thoughts affect our emotions. A simple thought about a person or a place affects how we *feel*. The will is our decision-making mechanism. And what we decide to do (will) for the most part is dictated by how we feel. Our actions produce our results in life. If you want to change a particular result, you have to work your way backward, determining what thought made you feel a certain way that led you to take a certain action. Once the thought is identified you can decide how to manage it and what to do about it. If you started working on your feelings in an attempt to change your results, you would be dealing with the symptoms and not the root cause. Each part of our being is intricately connected, and one part affects the others greatly.

When your purpose is unleashed, you can meet any challenge head-on. It is important that you don't give up in the seeking process! The authors of *The Power of Focus* encourage us in this pursuit:

> So press on with the search. Strive to understand more about yourself and the role you were designed to play. It is a journey...Along the way you will need to become more accountable. This requires making different choices...[4]

Often people find themselves wondering about their purpose. However, not all of them take the time to search, listen and learn. Obviously, you're not one of them!

5. GAIN A SOUND UNDERSTANDING

With so many odd teachings about the meaning of life's purpose out there, many individuals end up more confused and demoralized when they do attempt to discover it. A sound understanding is vital to discover our life purpose. You need to have a firm grip on it. To this end, I have dedicated several chapters of this book to exploring the different philosophical views regarding purpose, as well as some common misconceptions.

I have searched books that refer to "purpose" in their title or sub-title. My experience has been that a very small percentage of the content actually addresses the subject.

> *It would be difficult to live out our purpose without first making peace with ourselves.*

In dealing with this subject, there are some words that authors and teachers use interchangeably, leaving many people a bit confused. Some of these words are purpose, destiny, mission, vision and calling. Although some of these words are synonymous, for clarity, throughout this book, I use the word *purpose* to explain the *reason* for your existence.

The benefits obtained by discovering your purpose outweigh its requirements.

6. BE AT PEACE WITH YOURSELF

It would be difficult to live out our purpose without first making peace with ourselves.

One of the many blessings of discovering our purpose is the sense of significance it provides. How can I experience that sense of worth and meaning if I cannot value and accept myself the way God created me?

We are at total peace with ourselves when we get to the point of fully accepting:

- The color of our skin, eyes and hair
- Our stature
- The pitch of our voice
- Our facial features
- Our family

- Our nationality
- The geographical part of the world we are born into
- The window of time we are born in

If it were necessary for me to have been born in a different part of the world or at a different point in time to fulfill my purpose, it would have been so. But that's not the case. I was made in Heaven, packaged in Central America and delivered to the bosom of a Salvadorian family! I am not *out of* time either. I was born in the 1970s because this is the window of time that God has allotted me to live in to fulfill my life purpose. He has equipped me for this point in time, and I don't regret not being born in a different part of the world, or to a different family, or at another point in time.

Being at peace with self is looking into the mirror, loving and fully accepting every square inch of your glorious body, your soul and your spirit man. When you look into someone's eyes, you may see and perceive things about that person. You may even be able to discern some things, but many remain hidden.

Nothing is reserved when you look at yourself in the mirror. No one can look into your eyes and see all that *you* see. You are the one who can discern sadness, turmoil, self-doubt or dissatisfaction. However, when you have made peace with yourself, you see joy, peace, self-confidence, satisfaction and passion for life!

MIRROR EXERCISE

If possible, before you continue any further, I would like to invite you to do this exercise. Preferably, get in a private and quiet place where you can access a mirror. Look into the mirror, but not as you normally do to check your hair or make up. This look will be different from all the previous ones. Your eyes are the window of your soul. That is what you want to access. Look deeply and let your eyes reveal what is beyond them. This exercise is very powerful and it can furnish important information about the way you view yourself, and whether or not, you have fully accepted who you are.

If there are parts of you that you haven't fully accepted, please seek competent help to address them. As we were growing up, most of us were teased and made fun of for one reason or another. It is amazing how nicknames and verbal offenses can change the way we see and feel about ourselves. If we don't deal with these issues, they can have a detrimental effect on us, even as adults. Peace with yourself is never achieved by listening to the voice of your critics, but rather by seeing yourself through the eyes of your Designer!

> *Peace with yourself is never achieved by listening to the voice of your critics, but rather by seeing yourself through the eyes of your Designer!*

After identifying any issues and dealing with them, repeat this exercise and make note of any changes in the way you feel about yourself. The objective here is to identity any potential areas that may hinder you from having a healthy self-image.

To be at peace, you will need to like yourself. Malphurs addresses this subject:

> A second personal benefit of *knowing* who we are is *liking* who we are. There are far too many Christians who struggle with poor self-esteem, because when they look in a mirror they don't like what they see...Yet, in such passages as Ephesians 5:28-29, 33, Scripture speaks of loving ourselves in a positive light. A vital key to loving ourselves biblically, is liking ourselves...[5]

Moses had many self-image issues when God revealed his purpose to him. This is the reason that Moses cited so many personal inadequacies and attempted to dissuade God from sending him to deliver the people of Israel.

When you are at total peace with yourself and purpose looks into your eyes and says, "Thank you for diligently seeking me! I have been waiting for you. Now let's go make it happen," you will be ready. You won't put it on hold. Your answer will be a resounding, "Yes! I am ready. Let's do it!"

CHAPTER 8

RIPE OR UNRIPE?

As a reader of this book, you fit into one of two categories — the *ripe* or the *unripe*.

The ripe are those who are ready to discover their life purpose and only need a little bit of coaching. Life experiences may have already prepared them to discover it. They think about life's purpose very often. If that is your case, this book may be just the push you need to discover it. You may be closer to discovering your purpose than you think. It is highly possible that by the time you finish reading this book you will have discovered it, and even have a written life purpose statement. *That* is exciting!

As part of my research, I interview people almost on a daily basis. I share this topic with them and then ask a couple of questions. An example of a common question I ask is, "When was the last time you thought about what your purpose in life might be?"

As I was taking some time off with my family in east Texas, we ran across a woman and her fifteen-year-old daughter at a store. The teenager responded to my question by saying that she had entertained this very question that morning and that she normally thought about it at least three times per week. Barbara was able to provide an answer without much effort because it remained fresh in her mind. This is an example of people who fall in the *ripe* category. They meditate on this matter very often. When the question surfaces in their mind, they don't disregard it immediately. The desire to know their life purpose becomes much more important to them. They are the kind of people who won't be satisfied until they discover it.

The second category, which I call *unripe*, refers to people who haven't given a great deal of time to this matter. If asked about the last time they wondered about their purpose, they find it difficult to answer. They often make up an answer just so they won't feel embarrassed. If this is your case, this book will assist you by giving you the tools and the right frame of mind regarding purpose. It will prepare you by provoking and inspiring you to make your own discovery. It will start you on the wonderful path of unveiling what you were created to do, so that you can experience the power of living life on purpose.

CHAPTER 9

SEEKING IN THE
WRONG PLACES

Often people try to find their life purpose in the wrong places.

This is so true, especially with a self-destructing epidemic that plagues our society. I am referring to the wave of gangs found in just about every corner of the globe. Some of these have become international organizations that control pockets of the society in many countries.

These organized gangs never seem to have problems meeting their recruiting goals. Kids as young as eight years old, as well as older adults, form part of these organized groups. Their primary motivation is seeking to fill a desire deep inside them—a desire of belonging and of personal significance. They don't join just to be a part of that gang. They never say, "I'm part" of a gang. They say, I "belong" to a particular gang. Brutal rivalries exist among them. They are ready and willing to perform all the tasks that are demanded of them by the regional and local leaders.

Members are highly praised among their groups as they carry out delinquent tasks such as selling drugs, robberies, assaults, rapes and even murders. They live for these atrocities because the more they engage in them the more respect they gain among their peers and the higher they climb in the ranks. Part of what they are seeking is meaning and purpose. They have boarded the wrong *vehicle*.

I speak about this subject because in the past I have worked with many people who were gang members and managed to depart, many in one piece and others with many marks on their bodies.

Personally, I was one of the fortunate ones to depart, with many bumps and bruises, but in one piece. During my teen years, moved by a desire for meaning and fulfillment in life, I fell into the deception of this trap. I thought that this vehicle was the most accessible answer that society offered me at that moment. It was cheap, easy to belong to, and available in every corner of my neighborhood. I thought I had found what I was looking for: meaning, acceptance and fulfillment. *Acceptance*: I could dress, act and be whomever I wanted to be, a behavior that was encouraged not rejected. *Meaning*: I belonged to something that helped me define who I was. Overall, it gave me a sense of belonging and satisfaction, as I was seeking for meaning in life.

By no means am I excusing the appalling acts of violence committed by these individuals. I am simply pointing out that most people who engage in such activities do so in search of *meaning* and *belonging*. It is obvious that they are not living on purpose and they desperately need to be guided in the right direction.

By the time I was nineteen, I had been heavily involved in gang activities, selling illegal substances and firearms. Totally in the grip of the power of darkness, I had lost all respect for my parents and for everyone else. I just wanted to run the streets of Langley Park,

Washington D.C., and Virginia. Somehow, I graduated from High Point High School in Beltsville, Maryland. I had no desire or vision to further my education. I lived in the moment. I couldn't see beyond the present day because I never knew if I would be alive tomorrow.

Tuesday night about 8:45pm in the evening of December 4, 1990 forever changed the course of my life. My parents were supporting a pastor who was starting a church in Langley Park, Maryland. They had rented the cafeteria of Langley Park McCormick Elementary School to hold meetings on Tuesdays, Thursdays and Sundays. My graceful mother invited me to their first service. Reluctantly, I decided to go concluding that I would do it just to please my parents. In some way, I will survive, I thought! I figured that if I satisfied them by going to church they would leave me alone, and I could continue my lifestyle. Things didn't go as I planned!

I recall the moment when one of the pastors made an altar call. I kept my face hidden from his view. The pastor insisted. After a few moments, all of a sudden I found myself standing. I remember looking back to see if it had been one of the ushers who had pulled me out of my seat because I was ready to punch his lights out! However, there was no one behind me. I found myself walking out of the area where I was seated and making my way down the aisle towards the altar where the pastor was fervently inviting me to accept Jesus into my life. I kept on shaking my head saying no, I didn't want to do this. Yet, a force that was greater than I was pulling me towards the altar. I later learned that it was the power of God pulling me with his ropes of love towards Him.

At about five feet from the altar, I fell flat on my face. It felt as though a ton of bricks fell on my head and pushed me flat on the floor. I found myself in front of the altar with my face on the floor sobbing and weeping like a baby. I was confused. I kept on hearing voices say, "You're macho! What is wrong with you? You cannot do this life. You can't live without all the women, the nightclubs, and the money from the drugs." But, it wasn't me that had led me to the altar. It was God Himself who had pulled me towards Him. His power was much greater than my pride and rebellion.

I remember praying, "God, I don't know what is happening to me. But I ask you to forgive me of my sins. And if my life is any good to you, here it is."

I got up from the floor about fifteen minutes later, and so many things inside me had changed miraculously! I felt lighter! I felt the love of my brothers and sisters embracing me and rejoicing. I experienced the new birth. Seven months later, I started preaching the word of God in the local church, and soon it spread out to other states.

Sixteen years had passed after this life-changing experience. In September 2006, I embarked on my personal journey to discover my life purpose…and I found it. The months and years to come would unfold more revelation about the unique purpose that each one of us has. Inevitably, it became the topic of conversation in my home. During our "Power Conversations", when we speak about a Bible or personal growth topic with my wife and two daughters, I shared more and more about my findings. My life and that of my family has never been the same. We are a family of purpose, with purpose, and together we are living out our purpose. If God can take a person with a dark past such as mine, cleanse him, turn his life around, give him the joy of having a beautiful wife and daughters, and reveal His purpose, I have no doubt he can also do it for others!

I am grieved as I see the section of gangsters in our society because there is much potential in each one of these individuals. I have had the joy of meeting many men and women who left the streets and committed themselves to recovery and mentoring programs. What a difference they are making in their families and in society after restructuring their lives!

The gang life is just one example of the wrong places in which people tend to look for their purpose and come out empty handed. Certainly, many other similar places appeal to the masses that are looking for a sense of personal significance and self-worth. Other wrong places to look for purpose and significance include a social status, a relationship, a profession, and even sexual immorality. Unfortunately, all they offer is a substitute for the real thing.

The next section deals with the dominant philosophies of the meaning and purpose of life. It will guide you a step closer to find your own life purpose.

To maximize your time dedicated to this book, your participation is highly encouraged. You will find several exercises designed to assist you in discovering your purpose. It is my suggestion that you don't skip any of them. The first exercise is found on the next page. Please complete it before proceeding to part three.

Congratulations! You have just come one step closer in this worthy journey.

REFLECTION: INITIAL INVENTORY

Have I ever wondered what my life purpose is?

_____

_____

When was the last time I wondered about it?

_____

_____

Where was I the last time I entertained this question?

_____

_____

Normally, how long do I dwell on it when the question surfaces my mind?

_____

_____

How often does this question surface my mind?

_____

_____

_____

Generally, what events or circumstances prompt me to ask this question?

_____

_____

What have I done in terms of pursuing an answer for this question?

_____

_____

Please check ONE of the following

☐ Currently, I have no clue what my life purpose is. However, I am firmly persuaded that I will discover it very soon!

☐   At this point in my life I am not 100% sure what my life pur-
    pose is. However, I have an idea, and it is the following:

    _____

    _____

    _____

☐   I know my life purpose. My life purpose statement is the follow-
    ing:

    _____

    _____

    _____

Part 3

Six Dominant Philosophies

"So the human race is writing its story, finding itself, discovering its own underlying purpose, revising, recasting a tale pathetic often, yet nonetheless sublime."[1]

—Felix Adler

SIX DOMINANT PHILOSOPHIES

Different schools of thought in our society attempt to define meaning and purpose in life. We see it in the fashion, music and entertainment industries. To a great extent, these industries shape how youngsters attempt to define who they are by what they wear, the music genres they listen to and the entertainment venues they choose. The influence these industries gain in our society, especially with teenagers, is enormous!

One can belong to so many different cliques. These cliques provide teens various options to choose from and identify with. As a result, many teens feel so out of place that they face problems with personal identity and self-esteem. Some of them end up like Marty, the zebra in the movie *Madagascar,* who had lived all his life in a New York zoo and constantly dreamed about going into the wild. He was at a point where he didn't know if he was "white with black stripes or black with white stripes." Identity crisis is one big dilemma in our society.

The following is an excerpt from the movie *The Matrix Reloaded,* in which Agent Smith confronts Neo, and they have a conversation about the nature of purpose:

Agent Smith: But, as you well know appearances can be deceiving which brings me back to the reason why we're here. We're not here because we're free; we're here because we're not free. There's no escaping reason, no denying purpose because as we both know, without purpose we would not exist.

Smith 1: It is purpose that created us.

Smith 2: Purpose that connects us.

Smith 3: Purpose that pulls us.

Smith 4: That guides us.

Smith 5: That drives us.

Smith 6: It is purpose that defines.

Smith 7: Purpose that binds us.

Smith 1: We are here because of you, Mr. Anderson. We're here to take from you what you tried to take from us — purpose![2]

As we can see, our society, at different levels, is seeking for meaning and purpose. They too are attempting to provide some answers on this subject. I am sure that in some way these have helped people shape their ideas regarding life's purpose.

As the different philosophies are described, you may find out that your preconceived idea regarding purpose lines up with one of these. The reason for presenting the different philosophical perspectives regarding life's purpose is to clear the way so you can adapt a sound understanding about life's purpose. As explained earlier, your search for purpose is similar to looking for something of great value that you have misplaced.

POPULAR BELIEFS ABOUT PURPOSE

Prior to getting into the different philosophies, let us look at some common responses about the purpose of life.

1. To survive.

    What is the purpose of life? The purpose of life is to survive. Not for an individual to survive, but for an entire gene pool to survive.[3]

    To survive, including pursuit of indefinite lifespan (the closest thing to immortality that is theoretically possible) through scientific means.[4]

2. To evolve.

    The purpose of life is to evolve the mind to a point where you are making spirit choices, wise choices and decisions from the awakened perspective or the knowing within![5]

3. To succeed.

Success is really the fulfillment of goals and desires of any size or nature. Success is really living a life of meaning with the fulfillment of your particular natural talents, educated skills, and abilities. Success is the purpose of life. It is the natural aim of the human being to set goals and work to bring them into reality. It is how we grow and become more than we were, and it is in this that we find our purpose in life.[6]

4. To be Self-Identity.

The purpose of life is to be Self-Identity as Divinity created Self-Identity in its exact likeness, Void and Infinite.[7]

5. To seek happiness and flourish.
6. To enjoy life.
7. To experience pleasure and celebrate.
8. To acquire wealth.
9. To gain and exercise power.
10. To live every day as if it is your last and to do your best at everything that comes before you.
11. To always be satisfied.
12. To produce offspring through sexual reproduction.
13. To participate and contribute to a given society by going to school, working, paying taxes, being a good citizen, and contributing to raise the collective quality of life.
14. To advance technological evolution or to actively develop the future of intelligent life.
15. To compete or co-operate with others.
16. To destroy others who harm you.
17. To practice nonviolence and nonresistance.
18. To leave a legacy, such as a work of art or a book.
19. To eat.

20. To sleep.
21. To ensure that all others after you remember your name.
22. To prepare for death.
23. To spend life in the pursuit of happiness — maybe not to obtain it, but to pursue it relentlessly.
24. To protect and preserve one's kin, clan, or tribe.
25. To seek freedom, either physically, mentally or financially.
26. To observe the ultimate fate of humanity to the furthest extent possible.
27. To attempt to have many sexual conquests.
28. To find and take over all free space in this "game" called life.
29. To seek and find beauty.
30. To find and follow an artistic passion.
    (Popular beliefs 5-30 are from this source[8])

I am certain that you have heard at least a couple of these reasons in the past.

SIX DOMINANT PHILOSOPHIES

The way one attempts to define purpose in life is derived from one's philosophy about life itself. In my quest, I turned to varying literature. I found that many answers were generic and broad; others were vague to say the least. Yet others provided no incentive in discovering one's life purpose. Our society doesn't encourage people to discover it. There are relatively few sources one can turn to and feel persuaded to discover life's purpose.

After studying and researching different philosophies, I have summarized them into six categories:

1. Purpose is *Non-existent*
2. Purpose is *Common*
3. Purpose is *Universal*
4. Purpose is *Chosen*

5. Purpose is *Temporal*
6. Purpose is *Assigned*

By no means do I intend to present an in-depth view about each philosophy because it is not the primary focus of this book. I present an overview of these to assist you in discovering your own view of life's purpose and to clarify it, if needed. Let's take a brief look at each view.

CHAPTER 10

PURPOSE IS NON-EXISTENT

Bertrand Russell, a British philosopher once said, "Unless you assume a God, the question of life's purpose is meaningless."[1]

There are those who embrace the idea that there is no real purpose in life. You are born, you die, and it's over. The ones who ascribe to this idea are mostly those who don't believe in life after death or in the existence of God. I like the joke about the insomniac and dyslexic atheist who woke up in the middle of the night and was wondering if "dog" exists!

The philosophy that teaches that there is no purpose or meaning in life, lines up with the view of existential nihilism. Dr. Alan Pratt, chair of the general education program committee at the Embry-Riddle University in Daytona Beach, explains this philosophy:

> *Existential nihilism* is the notion that life has no intrinsic meaning or value...that the world is without meaning or purpose. Given this circumstance, existence itself — all action, suffering, and feeling — is

ultimately senseless and empty…. When we abandon illusions, life is revealed as nothing; and for the existentialists, nothingness is the source of not only absolute freedom but also existential horror and emotional anguish. Nothingness reveals each individual as an isolated being "thrown" into an alien and unresponsive universe, barred forever from knowing why, yet required to invent meaning… The common thread in the literature of the existentialists is coping with the emotional anguish arising from our confrontation with nothingness.[2]

If life has no meaning or purpose, its value may not be highly esteemed. Unfortunately, our culture has lost many values in recent decades; often it is referred to as a culture of death. Suicide and euthanasia are highly promoted. I was flabbergasted to know that many websites promote death and suicide. These provide detailed information about the best ways to commit suicide, the best weapons to use and the places and times to do it — a complete guide on checking out!

The following statistics are staggering. According to the Center for Disease Control, suicide took the lives of more than 33,000 people in 2006, which amounts to one suicide every 16 minutes. In 2007, emergency departments treated 395,320 people for self-inflicted injuries [suicide attempts]. Suicide is the third leading cause of death among young people ages 15-24.[3]

> *A philosophy that teaches that purpose is non-existent will undoubtedly diminish the value of life.*

Our society has become acclimated to the daily tragedies of suicides and homicides because the value of human life has been degraded.

A philosophy that teaches that purpose is non-existent will undoubtedly diminish the value of life. As a result, suicide and homi-cide rates are likely to increase.

CHAPTER 11

PURPOSE IS COMMON

We all don't share the same life purpose.

Some believe the idea that purpose is common to all people. They give a few across-the-board reasons for one's existence. I believe that this philosophy limits and denies the individuality and uniqueness for which every single one of us were created.

In my observation, this view is more prevalent in religious circles. Some of the most common reasons cited for purpose include to love God, to serve God, to worship and to preach.

If these are actual purposes for which some individuals exist, does it mean that people whose purpose isn't one of these four are exempt from loving God, serving Him, worshipping or preaching? For instance, you may not be able to carry a tune. Are you exempt from worshipping? You may not be able to address an audience from a pulpit. Are you exempt from sharing the Gospel? Or, if you can carry a tune, does it mean that your life purpose is to worship? I believe that if your purpose was solely to worship, then you would have been created an angel, a seraphim or a cherubim. These magnificent spiritual beings are designed specially to render the Lord the best praise—so much, that they have immediate access to God and worship Him day and night. The book of Revelation 8:6-11 gives an account of four seraphim who worship the Lord day and night.

Worship, in itself, is not a purpose. As citizens of the Kingdom of God and as sons and daughters of God, we have both privileges and responsibilities. Through worship, we are privileged to experience the deepest level of intimacy with the Lord. No other experience can make us more intimate with Him than worship. While on earth, genuine worship is the climax of our experience with God. Loving and worshipping God is our highest privilege as citizens of the Kingdom. According to Deuteronomy 6:5, we have a commandment to love the Lord. And Jesus said that God is seeking true worshippers in John 4:23.

Serving the Lord amounts to serving others and sharing the good news of the Gospel, and it is not a purpose either. To serve is the responsibility of every believer who has confessed Jesus Christ:

"Go into all the world and preach the good news to all creation."
(Mark 16:15)

What if you are not a preacher or don't have any theological training to preach the Gospel, are you exempt from sharing the good news? Not really. You don't require formal training or a pulpit to "preach" the Gospel. In fact, you don't even need a church to preach. We all can share the good news with relatives, friends, co-workers, school peers, and those with whom we come in contact.

There is no doubt that many individuals share similar talents, dreams and passions. However, our uniqueness is something we must all cherish. Even if your purpose matches closely with someone else's, which is possible, the way you perform it is unique. Absolutely no one else can be you! There are people whose life purpose is very similar to ours and we often network with them to maximize resources.

Even identical twins aren't "identical." Their interests and personalities are not the same. I believe our Creator delights very much in designing each one of us so uniquely. In addition, it is a way to show off His unlimited power, diversity and love to all humanity.

Addressing the singularity of each person, Malphurs writes:

> Our divine design includes such things as our temperaments and our natural gifts, talents, and abilities. All of this constitutes our divine design or makeup, our special "wiring" or "chemistry." While Christians may have similar designs, no two Christians have the same design.[1]

The philosophy that purpose is common to all of us supports the idea that all men are created with one general purpose. It disregards the possibility that everyone's uniqueness may have some correlation to their individual life purpose.

CHAPTER 12

PURPOSE IS UNIVERSAL

This philosophy teaches that life has no discernable purpose and that as humans we must adopt a universal one.

This is a very sad and meaningless way of looking at life. It is no wonder that most individuals, who adopt such views, often find themselves disappointed or angry.

The following excerpt explains this belief in more detail:

So, life and our universe have no discernable purpose. Let us return to where we started this chapter and discuss what alternative purpose, if selected, might give us a vision that we can live with and, more importantly, live for. Life, as I have said, cannot be proven to be directed toward a purpose. Neither existing nor evolving is a purpose… But we need a purpose to rationally make the many moral decisions thrust upon us by scientific and technological advances. And **we need a universally accepted one** if we are to achieve any degree of unanimity. So, one must be contrived. A word of caution before we proceed in selecting a purpose to guide us, we must be careful not to separate ourselves from life. Past religions did this — humans held themselves different from, and superior to, all other forms of life. We know better than this, nowadays. Life itself is our parent. Other living entities are our siblings. We have no more, and no less, purpose for living than life itself has. Thus, whatever we select to be a purpose for humans must be a purpose that applies to all other living entities, including those beyond our planet.

What, then, do we choose to be our universal purpose? Given that there is no detectable purpose pre-designed into life or the universe, then, if we must have one, we must adopt a surrogate.

To my mind, the only viable option is **to support life's continual evolution and focus upon helping it to achieve an omnipotent ability.** Such a purpose is universal and rational; it is a purpose that will last as long as life itself lasts. It accommodates the whole of life, and shows that we care about more than just our own well-being. It declares that we value life for its own sake and think little about the death that must follow, taking it simply as the price to be paid for living.[1]

This view of life is similar to the one that teaches that purpose is non-existent. However, it differs because though it assumes that life has no discernable purpose, it seeks to adopt a universal one for all human beings. Adopting a universally accepted purpose will encounter many challenges because of the many philosophical views.

CHAPTER 13

PURPOSE IS CHOSEN

I don't choose my life purpose.

Choosing our own purpose is a humanistic perspective. According to the humanist manifestos published by the American Humanist Association, human purpose is something not inherent but instead something chosen by individuals *without* any supernatural influence. They claim that natural propensities may determine what sorts of purposes a person needs to pursue and that your natural talents and gifts determine your life purpose. They also believe the human race came into existence by evolution and that knowledge doesn't come from supernatural sources. Instead, it flows from human observations, experimentation and rational analysis preferably using scientific methods.[1]

On her website, Donna Leslie, a secular humanist, writes the following:

Your individual purpose is your choice. It doesn't have to be forever. It can be from day to day. One intention will lead to another; intention builds on itself. It can be helpful to forget for the time being what your purpose is here on earth in the larger sense and ask yourself when you wake up in the morning, what's my purpose here on earth today? Keep it simple. Practice setting intention in your day to day activities and it will become simpler to manifest larger intentions, year to year ... or lifetime to lifetime.[2]

Those who believe in karma and reincarnation maintain that since we live multiple lives, each life has different purposes and our soul chooses the purpose for that current life. Carol Adrienne writes the following:

It is a necessary condition that we are born with no conscious memory of what we set out to do. Why? If it's true that we do live many lifetimes, then each life has its own purpose and set of experiences. Some of those experiences are left unresolved. This is what the Eastern traditions call karma. Karma, obviously, is a multidimensional complex of forces beyond any simple explanation. Karma is action. An action has consequences. Our identity comes from past actions, which create memories. Those memories create desires, which give rise to new choices and new actions. Let's say, as an example, that in one life you were a talented musician who died at age eighteen in a drunken brawl over a woman. You never got the chance to develop your talent... that unresolved energy pattern still exists at the energetic level of your being, when you exist without a physical body in between earthly lives. This unfinished business or karma must be completed in another life... Your soul, selecting a purpose for your life, may choose to postpone working on this karma or may choose this lifetime to work through it.[3]

You can choose many things in life. For instance, if you suffered rejection or neglect as a child, you can opt to live for the rest of your life as a victim. On the other hand, you can also choose to take ownership of life and the environment that surrounds you. You can choose to live in the present and not allow those negative experiences to determine your current quality of life. This has to do with the choices we make and the way we handle adversity in life, but not with us choosing our own life purpose.

Purpose exists before the product does.

Whether it is an electronic device, a piece of furniture or a vehicle, they don't choose their purpose. Their designer assigns purpose to them before they are engineered or fabricated. Purpose exists before the product does.

For me to believe that I am the one who chooses my life purpose, I would also have to believe that I *created* or *designed* myself.

CHAPTER 14

PURPOSE IS TEMPORAL

This philosophy doesn't see beyond the present life.

This school of thought encourages individuals to achieve their goals, accumulate wealth and assets, and to contribute to society. It promotes that pursuing a career, raising a family, devoting oneself to a creative vocation or to a cause, and acquiring property are perhaps the most widespread of long-term purposes that make life meaningful. It is temporal in the sense that it focuses mainly on material things.

Those who adopt this idea may find themselves financially well-off, with their goals achieved, but maybe still not fully satisfied. Materially speaking they may lack nothing. However, they may discover that acquiring wealth and accomplishing their goals are not in themselves the answer for the meaning and fulfillment they seek. They can find their lives "filled" yet empty. It is one of the dichotomies of life.

This idea provides a meaning of purpose only from a material and temporal perspective. Here is an example of someone embracing two philosophies mentioned in this section — purpose is chosen and purpose is temporal:

> We are free to create a purpose for our own lives. That is true whether a person is religious or not. How you choose to factor in the idea of an afterlife is similarly up to you. Personally I find the idea of an afterlife unnecessary, unnatural and unsettling, so I've chosen to dispense with the idea altogether.[1]

Purpose is two-fold; when it is identified properly, one is able to see that it has its place and time on earth *and* in eternity. Part 6 will cover more about this topic.

CHAPTER 15

PURPOSE IS ASSIGNED

God has created us with a specific purpose in life.

Purpose goes beyond this life and beyond our natural talents and gifts. It has an eternal effect. It influences the earthly and the temporal, as well as the supernatural and the eternal.

When you identify your life purpose properly, it will line up with the earthly and temporal, as well as with the supernatural and eternal. In other words, your purpose lines up with God's supreme purpose. Referring to this philosophy, Robert Morris adds:

> In order to discover the purpose that God has for your life, you must first believe that you have one! God created you for a unique purpose ... We know that God has an eternal purpose for everything ... But is important to know that you, as an individual, have a *specific purpose* as well. God has a unique destiny for you—and you are the only one that can fulfill it.[1]

FROM THE MOUTHS OF BABES

As we were driving to church on a Sunday morning, I asked my daughters what they thought was the reason so many people don't discover their life purpose. At that time, Gianna was six and Nathalia was four. The answers that came forth were amazing for their age. It is also very important for each person to embrace these truths in order to discover their purpose. Gianna said, "Daddy, I believe many people don't know their purpose because they don't know they are a treasure to the world!"

> *"Many people don't know their purpose because they don't know that they are a treasure to the world!"*
> *-Gianna Lima*

Her answer is so true, and it comes out of her values, respect for life and self-esteem. A healthy perspective in these areas is a must for anyone to discover and grow in their purpose. Most people you meet on a daily basis don't feel they are very special.

From my younger daughter's answer, you will be able to tell that she embraces the belief that God creates us, and He assigns purpose to our lives. Nathalia knows about the "human manufacturing plant!" Her answer was, "Daddy, number one is because maybe they don't know God yet. And number two, because maybe they are not born yet and God hasn't given them their purpose yet."

This little one reached deep in the files of theology to come up with such answer. We were all in awe of what had come out of the mouth of these babes!

DESIGNED PURPOSELY

God designed each of the Biblical characters for a specific purpose. Each was strategically born in their proper time and age. They had special qualities and inclinations that were clues about their purpose. Initially, some of these individuals couldn't visualize themselves living out their purpose as God revealed it to them. Actually, they argued with God as in was the case with Moses, Jonah and Jeremiah. The reason for their resistance was mostly due to a feeling of inadequacy. They felt that they didn't meet the requirements and demands of their task.

Did God make a mistake assigning their purpose, or they just couldn't discern it at that moment? The latter is correct. As they grew into their purpose, gradually they gained more confidence and finally settled with the fact that God had designed them purposely. They embraced this fact wholeheartedly and made history as they lived out their divine design.

EMBRACING PURPOSE

Exodus chapters three and four relate the account when God revealed his purpose to Moses — to be a *deliverer* for the Israelites. Moses presented excuse after excuse in an attempt to convince God that he wasn't the person cut out for this job. Here are some excuses he cited:

- The *no reputation* excuse, "who am I to...?" (Exodus 3:11)
- The *they don't know you* excuse, "If they ask me, what is his [God's] name?" (Exodus 3:13)
- The *what if* excuse, "what if they do not believe me or listen to me?" (Exodus 4:1)
- The *I am incapable* excuse, "I have never been eloquent ... I am slow of speech and tongue." (Exodus 4:10)

Moses tried hard to get out of this assignment. The reason for his opposition was that he was not in *alignment* with the *inside* (Personal design), the *outside* (Life experiences), and *above* (Life purpose).

It is amazing how the lack of awareness concerning these areas in life can inhibit you from discerning your life purpose. Moses possessed natural qualities and abilities that were completely adequate for the task. Additionally, life had already prepared him through personal and spiritual experiences. Moses had lived as a prince and as a fugitive. His father in law, Jethro, was the priest of Midian. Moses had a genuine concern for those who were oppressed. He couldn't stand injustice, which at times, had gotten him in trouble. His life purpose would bring much needed clarification even to some of his most difficult past experiences. Yet, when God revealed His purpose to Moses, initially he objected. He seemed to be unable to *connect* the dots.

Eventually, Moses yielded to God's purpose for him. At that moment, something remarkable happened. Moses aligned himself with his personal design, his life experiences and his life purpose — inside, outside and above. He became a different person! Life isn't the same when we are totally aligned with our personal design, our life experiences and our life purpose.

Later, Moses delivered the people out of Egypt. In the book of Exodus chapter thirty-two, we find an amazing account of Moses interceding on behalf of the Israelites as they had rebelled against God. The Israelites constantly murmured and complained about their journey through the desert. At times they wanted to stone Moses; at other times, they talked about choosing a new leader to take them back to Egypt. It was constant bickering and complaining.

While Moses was meeting with God in Mount Sinai for forty days, the Israelites decided to turn their allegiance to idols they created out of their own gold. They figured that Moses was taking too long and was probably already dead up in the mountain. God proposed the following solution to Moses:

> "I have seen these people," the LORD said to Moses, "and they are a stiff-necked people. Now leave me alone so that my anger may burn

against them and that I may destroy them. Then I will make you into a great nation." (Exodus 32:9-10)

This proposal doesn't sound bad considering all that Moses had endured with these stiff-necked fellows, does it? Well, if Moses hadn't fully embraced his purpose I believe he wouldn't have thought twice. However, by now Moses doesn't sound like the fellow attempting to persuade God that He had made a mistake by assigning him the task of bringing freedom to an oppressed people. The transformed Moses immediately disregards the idea of God destroying all the Israelites and raising

> *When you aligned yourself with your Designer's intention, your influence touches heaven and earth!*

a great nation out of him, even if this new nation wouldn't have any whiners! He fully understood and totally accepted his task. Moses knew that no one else was better equipped to carry it out. This is Moses' plea and the result he obtained:

> But Moses sought the favor of the LORD his God. "O LORD," he said, "why should your anger burn against your people, whom you brought out of Egypt with great power and a mighty hand? Why should the Egyptians say, 'It was with evil intent that he brought them out, to kill them in the mountains and to wipe them off the face of the earth?' Turn from your fierce anger; relent and do not bring disaster on your people. Remember your servants Abraham, Isaac and Israel, to whom you swore by your own self: 'I will make your descendants as numerous as the stars in the sky and I will give your descendants all this land I promised them, and it will be their inheritance forever.'" Then the LORD relented and did not bring on his people the disaster he had threatened. (Exodus 32:11-14)

Moses' attitude and intercession about this ordeal is evidence that he fully embraced his life purpose and developed appreciation for it. When you aligned yourself with your Designer's intention, your influence touches heaven and earth! Your voice is heard even in the heavenly courts.

Purposeless individuals will never affect the Kingdom of God. Those who fully accept and embrace God's purpose have a voice in the natural and spiritual realms.

Are you ready to influence the Kingdom of God? Are you out of alignment? Are you so concerned about your limitations that you can't see your strengths? Your unique personal and spiritual experiences have been preparing you for your individual task. Are you resisting or resenting your life purpose? If discovered in this journey, are you ready to embrace it?

God determines our life purpose; we discover and embrace it. Make the shift—embrace your divine design!

REFLECTION: PHILOSOPHIES

Which one of these philosophies (or combination of them) did I learn from my family as I was growing up?

_____

_____

Which one of the philosophies is prevalent among religious circles?

_____

_____

The philosophy that maintains that purpose has no supernatural influence is:

_____

_____

Which philosophy teaches that life has no discernable purpose?

_____

_____

I firmly believe in the following life purpose philosophy:

_____

_____

PART 4

MISCONCEPTIONS

"Unfortunately many people create all sorts of false barriers — or as I like to call them, 'glass ceilings' — that keep them from discovering and fulfilling God's purpose in their lives."

— Art Sepúlveda

MISCONCEPTIONS

Naturally, the environment in which we grow up influences us greatly and consequently shapes us in certain ways. It is here where we adopt part of our beliefs about matters such as politics, religion, family, sexuality, money and relationships.

Our parents, closest friends, teachers and culture also have great influence over us. The beliefs we adopt can be positive or negative. The flawed ideas that we embrace often can have a long lasting grip on us. We may find ourselves with constant problems when it comes to dealing with particular areas of our lives. To experience success in those areas, we have to trace our beliefs back to where and when we learned them. Then we have to *unlearn* them so we can embrace the truth with a correct understanding.

One widespread misconception is in regards to money. Anyone raised in a home where money was always scarce and a conflict-ridden topic, most likely will grow up with a misconstrued view about it. If most of what we heard while growing up sounded like "We can't afford it. What do you think I am... a bank? Money doesn't grow on trees." — then as adults, we would need to change the way we think about money drastically, if financial success is expected. Again, in a case like this, we would have to first *unlearn* what was instilled in us and then embrace the correct views of financial principles and stewardship.

So what does all of this have to do with discovering your purpose? We have picked up information from the same sources, either consciously or subconsciously. Just as we must correct misconstrued ideas regarding money in order to be financially successful, we must also identify and correct all misconceptions regarding purpose.

Many sources and voices speak on the subject of life's purpose. As noted previously, we often pick up a little bit of information from here and there. Then, whether consciously or subconsciously, we adopt our thoughts and beliefs about this and many other subjects in life based on the information we receive. If this information has flaws, the concepts we adopt will also be flawed. Addressing some of these hurdles, Art Sepúlveda writes:

> Unfortunately many people create all sorts of false barriers — or as I like to call them, 'glass ceilings' – that keep them from discovering and fulfilling God's purpose in their lives. Because the ceilings are made of glass they often aren't aware of the barriers and cannot understand why they matter. As a result they drift along in life feeling as they have no purpose or value.[1]

This section will address four common misconceptions regarding life's purpose. Pay special attention to those you may identify with, so you can correct them, if needed. This clarity will take you a step closer in the discovery of your life purpose.

CHAPTER 16

IS DEFINED BY AN OCCUPATION

By far, attempting to identify life's purpose by a profession or trade is the most prevalent misconception.

WHAT DO YOU DO FOR A LIVING?

When asked about their life purpose, almost invariably, people discuss their occupation. The primary reason is that since our childhood we were asked what we wanted to *be* when we grew up. We gave such answers as doctor, teacher, lawyer, and a whole range of other professions. Since an early age, we started to connect our *desired occupation* with *who* we are. We started to learn to identify *what we do* with *who we are*. We became conditioned to think that a profession *(our desired occupation)* describes our purpose *(who we are)*.

Even now as adults when we meet someone for the first time, one question that pops up almost always is, what do you do for a living?

Why do we ask this question? Is it curiosity? Is it to break the ice? I believe it goes beyond that. People get a level of significance from their jobs. Usually we will be asked the same question, and we will have our turn to respond. I believe the primary reason that question is asked so often is that subconsciously we tend to define people by their occupation. In the same way, we also tend to portray who we *are* by what we *do*.

People answer this question in different ways. For example, a civil engineer may respond by saying that he is in the engineering industry, while another one may say, "I am a civil engineer". When one says *I am* an engineer, doctor, lawyer ... it causes us to link who he *is* with what he *does*. The profession or trade is defining who that individual is. We do this subconsciously.

Personally, I have been involved in different professions in my life. I have been in information technology (IT) and in the mortgage industry. I have been an employee and a self-employed entrepreneur. If I was to attempt to link my purpose with my involvement in the mortgage industry, this is what it would look like: When God created Nestor Lima He created Nestor to be a mortgage broker. That would be so shallow. I have nothing against this particular industry; in fact, I enjoyed assisting families get into their homes. However, when it comes to defining life's purpose, any profession, regardless of how elite or noble it may be, will always fall short in defining an individual's purpose. No profession or trade has the ability to define our purpose and to provide the meaning and significance we all long for.

Imagine if your purpose in life was to be whatever the occupation you have pursued, such as a dentist, chiropractor, gynecologist, lawyer, surgeon, teacher, or an auto mechanic. Try saying, "I was created to be a _____ (fill in your profession or trade)." Does it satisfy your quest for your purpose? I am doubtful that it does. No trade or profession has the ability to do that.

Keep in mind that nowadays graduating with a double or even triple major is very common. The primary motivation is the ability to operate in different professions. After graduating, if one doesn't enjoy the chosen industry, there is always that second one to try out. Professions or trades change — purpose does not. In fact, you can live out your purpose in whatever profession or trade you operate.

> *Professions or trades change—purpose does not.*

Nowadays, some students change their major a time or two during their college years. They may even change it a few more times, if someone else is paying for them. As a result, they may end up "cramming" four years into five or even six!

In our present day, by the time people reach twenty-five it is possible they will have worked in at least five different industries. When I reached this age, I had done the following: landscaping, cleaning offices, bagging groceries, grocery department manager, shipping and receiving clerk, auto technician and copier technician. Later, I went into the computer industry as a network administrator, followed by the mortgage and real estate industries. Imagine just how confused I would be if I attempted to identify my life purpose in light of my diversity of occupations!

What then, does the profession or trade have to do with one's purpose? What about my natural talents and abilities, do they have any connection at all? If my occupation doesn't define my purpose, why should I work? Let us explore these questions.

The answer to these questions comes by realizing that while our occupation is not our purpose, it may be a *vehicle* to live it out. An occupation has the ability to provide a platform for you to exercise your purpose. You can earn a living pursuing the profession of your choice, so you might as well choose something you enjoy doing. You can earn money washing dishes, mowing lawns, performing surgical procedures or legally representing a client.

The great Apostle Paul was aboard an incorrect vehicle for a good part of his life. He thrived persecuting Christians and dragging them to jail. This is what he lived for. He was greatly feared everywhere he went. Having received written authority, he journeyed to Damascus to apprehend the Christians who lived and worshiped in that city. On his way there, he had a vivid encounter with Jesus, and his life was forever changed. His life purpose statement is found in the following Scripture:

"Go! This man is my chosen instrument to carry my name before the Gentiles and their kings and before the people of Israel." (Acts 9:15)

When Paul passed through what I call the human manufacturing plant, he was sealed with the purpose of "Carrying the Lord's name before the Gentiles and their kings and before the people of Israel" (Acts 9:15). It took him a while to discover it, but he did. The Bible also says that he was a tent maker; he had to work to eat. His occupation was in the construction industry. I don't see a connection between what he did for a living with his life purpose. His trade didn't define what his purpose was. However, I am sure he lived out his purpose as he built new places for people to live in, whether they were Jews or Gentiles.

Living life on purpose gives you a new perspective about life and about adversities experienced along the way. Paul was sent to jail many times and he would start singing. He knew that even a trip to jail was an opportunity to live out his purpose. Only during these occasions, he had the opportunity to carry the name of Jesus to the kings, which was part of his purpose. When he appealed his case to King Agrippa, the king confessed to Paul that he was almost persuaded to become a Christian (Acts 26:28).

In addition to Paul, many other Bible characters had vocations unrelated to their life purpose. For example, Matthew was a tax collector, Luke was a doctor, Peter was a fisherman, Moses was devoted to grazing sheep, and Nehemiah was the cupbearer to the king. Jesus was a carpenter. Their vocations never dictated their life purpose.

If, consciously or subconsciously, you have attempted to define your purpose with your profession, it is now time for a paradigm shift. Remember that God created man long before man assigned different titles and designations for occupations, which define *what* people *do*, not *who* they *are*. Many people use their professions as a means to finance what they truly love to do. Some of them eventually find themselves leaving their field of work to be dedicated completely to their purpose. This is a worthy goal!

DECLARATION

My profession or trade does not define my life purpose. However, it may serve as a vehicle or platform for me to live it out!

CHAPTER 17

IS DEFINED BY NATURAL TALENTS AND GIFTS

What about natural talents and gifts — do they define our purpose?

Many people are born with a special gift in such areas as music, math, science, comedy, sports, leadership, and the list goes on. I am gifted in soccer and in just about any sport. Does this mean that I was created with the purpose of being a soccer player or an athlete?

In any sport, there is great risk of permanent injury. We have seen football players who, after tackling another player, have remained bound to a wheelchair for the rest of their days. If their talent or ability defined their life purpose, one could conclude that it has ended.

As with professions or trades, athletes also change their preference of sports. Does this mean that their purpose has changed? Natural talents and abilities may change depending on the season of your life — purpose remains constant.

Although natural talents or abilities don't define my purpose, they may be closely related. In addition, they may provide both a clue to discover it and a platform to live it out. Robert Morris clarifies this effectively:

> An important key to understanding your purpose can be found in discovering the gifts God has given you. Remember, God has designed you with a purpose in mind. So the gifts He has given you will always be related to your purpose in some significant way ... they will tell you a lot about your purpose. Those gifts can help you understand your destiny in God.[1]

A. C. Green is a great example of someone who uses the platform of a professional athlete to live out his purpose. He is an NBA champion, mentor, speaker, author and a successful businessman. He played for the Los Angeles Lakers, the Dallas Mavericks, the Phoenix Suns and the Miami Heat. Green is noted for his record of the most consecutive games played in the history of the NBA, namely 1,192 games. In addition, he is recognized for his decision to remain abstinent until he got married at age thirty-nine. Green's mission is, "to help young people build self-esteem and character, and learn moral and ethical principles which will help them make responsible decisions."[2]

Green speaks in schools and churches around the country, sharing his message of abstinence. He has written a six-week curriculum on abstinence entitled *I've Got the Power,* along with a workbook entitled *Game Plan,* which addresses the same topic. We can see that his purpose is not necessarily to be a basketball player. However, those same skills paved the way for him to live out his purpose. Green writes:

> I believe that my position as an NBA star is a platform from which

to be heard, and a vehicle to help young people.[3]

This is just one example of many who are using their talents or professions to carry out their life purpose — it is not limited to the sports arena.

John C. Maxwell provides an account of a journalist who told the story of three construction workers:

"What are you doing?" he asked the first worker. "I am earning a check," he grumbled. The reporter asked the same question of a second laborer, who looked over his shoulders and said, "What does it look like I'm doing? I am pouring concrete." Then he noticed a third man who was smiling and whistling as he worked. "What are you doing?" he asked the third worker. He stopped what he was doing and said excitedly, "I'm building a shelter for the homeless." He wiped his hands clean on a rag and then pointed, "Look, over there is where the kitchen will be. And that over there is a women's dormitory..."[4]

All three of the workers were doing the same job, but only the third one was motivated by a greater vision. The work he was performing was fulfilling his purpose and added value to his efforts.

When you discover your purpose, you must start where you are and work with what you have. You will learn that you can live out your purpose even in your current working environment.

CHAPTER 18

NOT EVERYONE CAN
DISCOVER IT

There is an unspoken belief that not every person has the ability to discover their purpose. This belief, in a sense, supports the philosophy that purpose is non-existent.

It is true that a great number of people go to the grave without ever living out their life purpose. It is a sad truth. We see teenagers overdose and people engaged in self-destructive habits that basically render their lives non-operational. The great question is; do they have a life purpose? Can they discover it? The answer is yes to both. A person in such a situation has a purpose, but it is obvious they are not living it—and neither can they find it unless a change in lifestyle occurs.

When I was a gangster, running the streets of Langley Park, Maryland and Washington D.C., I had the same purpose as I do now. In fact, now that I look back I realize that I always had a desire to build up people whether it was making them better basketball players on the court or better street fighters.

I loved to instill confidence in my basketball and soccer teammates. Whenever we played basketball, often I would let the other team choose the better players. I would quickly notice the weaknesses of my players and start building them up by expressing my confidence in them and showing them the adjustments they needed to make. I didn't emphasize nor dwell on their mistakes. If they missed a shot, I encouraged them by telling them that they would get it the next time they tried. It wasn't unusual for us to beat another team that had an advantage over us. Normally, I would see the opposite on the other team. If one made a mistake, everybody would jump on him.

When I was a gangster, I had the same purpose as I do now.

On a certain occasion, I went to play at the basketball court near my home. There were two other guys and a girl already playing. We wanted to play two-on-two so I ended up with the girl as my teammate. In a matter of minutes, my teammate's game had improved tremendously. We ended up winning all three games we played, and she scored most of the points!

My life purpose now is the same as I had while I was living the lifestyle of a gangster. The reason I couldn't find it during that season in my life is because, number one, I wasn't seeking it, and number two, the environment and lifestyle I lived was unsuitable. The fact that a certain lifestyle may be inadequate for discovering one's purpose doesn't negate purpose or the ability to find it—it just calls for some changes.

In our home, the conversation about purpose and personal growth is very common. My wife, Dina, asked me one day, "Why is it that finding one's purpose isn't something natural or automatic?" It is a great question. Sometimes I wish it was like puberty so we would have a good idea about the age when it occurs.

Consider how different it would be if there was a *natural* age when we discovered our life purpose. Imagine if it was in the twenties, or in the thirties, or the sixties, then each of us would feel differently depending on where we are in the spectrum. Purpose is to be pursued and desired, if it occurred by an automatic process, it would eliminate the great rewards of its discovery.

Many people are not too concerned with the subject until they approach their forties or even fifties. This fact doesn't mean they have to wait until then. I don't think there is a minimum age, within reason, for people to discover their purpose. Our daughters discovered their life purpose at ages four and six. I understand this is unusual, but they have been exposed to information that many of us didn't have at that age. In my home, the topics of purpose and unlocking God's greatness inside us, is our daily bread.

CHAPTER 19

IS NOT THAT IMPORTANT

The idea that purpose isn't very important is an unconscious belief many people adopt. What we pursue in life is greatly influenced by our upbringing.

We often hear about multi-generations that have pursued a particular profession or trade. Some of our current military men and women can trace their family's service to this nation a few generations back. There are companies that have been family-owned for many decades. The reason is clear. For example, if a family owns an auto dealership, by the time their child is ten years old he may know a great deal about the business. I have heard six- or seven-year-old kids doing radio commercials for auto dealerships and other businesses with their parents. In this manner they are being introduced to the business. They learn to speak what they hear their parents speak. This will inevitably influence what they pursue later in life. To these children, their family business is important.

If as children or young adults we heard very little to nothing about discovering one's purpose, we can subconsciously succumb to a belief that this aspect of life is *not* very important. Our reasoning is that if it were important, our parents (or guardians) would have emphasized it!

Purpose is a topic I cannot recall ever exploring with my family as I was growing up. There were many other good things we were taught, such as respect, hard work and being a good citizen. However, if I were to measure the importance of life's purpose by what I was taught about it at home, it wouldn't rank at the top.

Not teaching our children about the importance of living on purpose produces the belief that purpose is not an important aspect of life.

We as parents make a concerted effort to teach our children those values and things that we feel will serve them well in life. If the importance about living on purpose is not included, it will not become part of their persuasions as they develop.

The following quote demonstrates a disinterested attitude towards life's purpose: "My life has no purpose, no direction, no aim, no meaning, and yet I'm happy. I can't figure it out. What am I doing right?"[1]

As my family and I were having lunch at an Italian restaurant on a particular occasion, our younger daughter, who was four at that time, asked the waitress if she knew her life purpose. The waitress was stunned at the question, and she responded honestly that she didn't know it. After she walked away, Nathalia turned to my wife and me with a shocked look in her face, "I can't believe that she doesn't know her purpose, and I know mine and I am only four!"

Nathalia was far more surprised than the waitress was! Up until then Nathalia believed that everyone knows their purpose, especially adults, because it is something so natural and important to her.

Not teaching our children about the importance of living on purpose produces the belief that purpose is not an important aspect of life. This is reinforced by the silence in our society on this topic.

Attempting to discover purpose under any of these misconceptions always produces an empty result. These empty results will in turn produce frustration, regardless of your sincere desire to know it. These misconceptions need to be replaced with sound truths.

In the next part, I will guide you one step closer to your purpose discovery by laying a strong foundation.

REFLECTION: MISCONCEPTIONS

What do you think your parents considered the most important subject they taught you in life, and how did they address it?

_____

_____

How important would you say your parents considered life's purpose?

_____

Before reading this section of the book, had you ever felt that discovering your life purpose was almost impossible? How do you feel about it now?

_____

Which misconceptions regarding purpose presented in this section, consciously or subconsciously, had you adopted in the past?

_____

_____

How do these misconceptions hinder you in the process of discovering your life purpose?

_____

_____

How does clarifying and understanding these misconceptions help you in the process of discovering your life purpose?

_____

_____

PART 5

LAYING
THE
FOUNDATION

"Your eyes saw my unformed body. All the days ordained for me were written in your book before one of them came to be."

Psalm 139:15-16

LAYING THE FOUNDATION

The big question, "What is my purpose in life?" has echoed in the hearts of the most brilliant minds known to humankind as well as those not considered so great, the wealthy and educated, the poor and illiterate.

As humans, we differ in many things that go beyond nationality, culture and religion. The need for meaning and purpose is among those *common* needs we all share. The reason many hop on the wrong vehicle in life is that they are seeking for meaning, acceptance and fulfillment. The mere fact that people seek answers about their purpose is a confirmation that purpose exists, not just *in* life, but also *for* our individual lives.

We have covered some exciting reasons for discovering our purpose, the different philosophical stands, and the misconceptions. Overcoming these hurdles is essential in this pursuit as it prepares the way for a real encounter with your life purpose.

This chapter will lay out the fundamental principles. A solid launching pad is required so that we can take off safely toward our destination. A safe take-off increases the possibility of a successful landing.

CHAPTER 20

SIGNIFICANCE
AND FULFILLMENT

As humans we have certain needs that when met make life much more enjoyable. Besides food, shelter and clothing, here is a list of what I consider to be the greatest needs human beings have: to be loved, to love, to be accepted (for who we are), to trust, to be trusted, to feel significant, and to feel fulfilled.

Love is a great need we all have. It would be so horrible if, in more than six billion people on earth no one loved me—not even one person! And it would be just as bad, if I had no one to love.

Trust is one of the greatest gifts anyone can give you and it is wonderful to have someone that you can trust also. People who don't give and partake of this gift live with a heightened sense of distrust. The gift of trust is priceless!

Another great experience in life is when we are simply accepted for who we are, which seems to be a rare experience. People are quick to voice their opinions and pass judgment about others at a simple glance. Others will try to change certain things about us without having the right to do so. The right to offer an opinion or to make a suggestion is earned by the investment of time and resources into a relationship. Just by looking on the surface, we don't know what changes a person has made to get their lives where they are today.

SOURCES OF SIGNIFICANCE

There are two sources of significance: stable and unstable.

Some sources from which we can derive certain degrees of significance include love, acceptance, trust, a profession or trade, a social status, a job, or a relationship—especially marital. These are good sources and can certainly make us feel better about ourselves. However, the main problem with them is their susceptibility to change. These sources are *subject to change* at any moment.

> *To truly enjoy the sense of worth and significance we all seek, we need to turn to a stable source.*

A person who says that he or she loves, accepts and trusts you deeply, can turn against you in a flash. A relationship can end due to death or disagreement. A profession or trade can be lost due to economic problems or technological advances. A social status can crumble due to a poor decision. A job can disappear overnight. I call these *unstable* sources of significance.

To truly enjoy the sense of worth and significance we all seek, we need to turn to a *stable* source—the kind that remains unwavering when we experience the loss of a certain social status, a job, or even a loved one. We need something that will support us even when everything around us falls apart. The only source that can provide such support is purpose. Purpose gives us identity; it defines the *core* of our being. Significance is highly derived from our identity. Your life purpose is the invisible umbilical cord that connects and identifies you with your Creator. This connection provides you the greatest sense of significance possible. Who you are is defined by whose you are. The external and unstable sources only define our profession, where we live, where we shop, what we wear and what we drive.

> *Your life purpose is the invisible umbilical cord that connects and identifies you with your Creator.*

We experience two main benefits when we discover our purpose. These are also the primary reasons we are concerned about discovering it: *significance* and *fulfillment*.

SIGNIFICANCE

Significance relates to our sense of personal importance and value — the knowing that we are *valuable* for something or for someone. Our pursuit for significance addresses our worth as individuals. People who lack a sense of meaning and fulfillment become very susceptible to feelings of insignificance, low self-esteem, inferiority and depression. The remedy for these symptoms cannot be procured at the local drug store. The best cure is the inner sense of meaning that comes as a result of properly identifying one's life purpose.

A particular status in society doesn't necessarily satisfy this quest. People in both high and low places are susceptible to self-destructive habits or tendencies such as drugs, alcohol, immorality or even suicide. The way we live our lives reveals the level of significance and worth we give ourselves. Through our actions, we broadcast how much we think we are worth.

One of the greatest gifts to humanity was an uncommon entrepreneur known as Mary Kay Ash. I cannot think of anyone who possessed a better understanding about our great need for feeling important. Mary Kay's ability to make individuals *feel* important was one of her greatest secrets in creating a multi-million dollar enterprise based on nurturing people with a personal human touch. She recounts a time when she attended a sales conference and waited in line for three hours to shake the vice president's hand. When she shook his hand, he said hello but didn't even look at her. Instead, he looked over her shoulders to see how many people were left in line. She felt as if she was invisible, and in her disappointment, she said to herself:

> If I am ever in a position where people stand in line to shake my hand, I am going to give each person my undivided attention, no matter how long the line is ... Now people stand in line to shake my hand on many occasions and I do my best to make every single person feel important ... there have been occasions when I had to shake hands with several thousand people. I am often asked how I do this without becoming utterly exhausted ... I keep in mind that each person in line has been waiting for as long as I have.[1]

In a chapter of her book, *You Can Have It All,* she writes about the "invisible sign." Here is how she explains this concept:

> I have learned to imagine an invisible sign around each person's neck that says, "Make me feel important!" Today I see this sign on everyone I meet and I respond to it immediately. I never cease to be amazed at how positively people react when they are made to feel important.[2]

We all need to feel special. Purpose gives us this feeling, and it is long lasting.

FULFILLMENT

Fulfillment brings us satisfaction, pleasure and joy. It has more to do with *what* we do than *who* we are. Whenever we have completed a task, especially one that required a significant amount of effort, we feel so pleased. There is no substitute for the degree of gratification experienced when we function directly *in* our purpose! Purpose gives us both the significance and the fulfillment we all desire in life, like nothing else does.

Significance and fulfillment are two primary reasons for our motivation to pursue and discover our life purpose. They are dynamite! It is uncommon to see a person living out his or her purpose and depressed at the same time. These two opposite feelings seldom coexist in those who know and live out their purpose.

Significance gives us peace and the sense of importance and personal worth. Fulfillment, on the other hand, provides happiness, joy, contentment, satisfaction, pleasure and gratification. This, in turn, produces a burning desire to impact the lives of others.

> *Purpose gives us both the significance and the fulfillment we all desire in life, like nothing else does.*

Your life purpose is the only unmovable, unshakeable, and unchangeable source for significance and fulfillment in life. All other sources are subject to change. From what source are you deriving your sense of significance today?

CHAPTER 21

DESIGNED ON PURPOSE

Everything created by God has a purpose!

When we look around creation, this becomes very evident. Trees exist for more than just decorating planet earth. The sun, the moon and the stars exist for predefined reasons. In addition to assigning purpose to all things, God also has blessed all his creation with glory. God wastes no resources—He is an artist. To illustrate, let us look at three fascinating characters in the Bible.

DAVID: THE PSALMIST

The Psalmist made the following profound declaration:

For you created my inmost being; you knit me together in my mother's womb. I praise you because I am fearfully and wonderfully made; your works are wonderful, I know that full well. My frame was not hidden from you when I was made in the secret place. When I was woven together in the depths of the earth, your eyes saw my unformed body. All the days ordained for me were written in your book before one of them came to be. How precious to me are your thoughts, O God! How vast is the sum of them. (Psalm 139:13-17)

Let's consider the following information about this scripture:

- **For you created my inmost being; you knit me together in my mother's womb!** (Verse 13)

  We are spirit, soul and body. The "inmost being" refers to the spirit man. This is the *essence* of mankind and the *eternal* part of man that God *communicates* with.

- **I praise you because I am fearfully and wonderfully made; your works are wonderful, I know that full well. How precious to me are your thoughts, O God! How vast is the sum of them!** (Verses 14 and 17)

  This describes the Artist at work and denotes a strong knowledge about the works of art of God. God invested time in our design and creation. There is a lot of creativity and ingenuity in our design.

- **My frame was not hidden from you when I was made in the secret place.** (Verse 15)

  The frame refers to our body structure, makeup and height, the color of our skin, eyes, hair, and the like. I am God's product. He is my designer, my engineer, my artist. I am His masterpiece! The Merriam Webster dictionary defines frame as: "something composed of parts fitted together and united; the physical makeup of an animal and especially a human body."[1]

- **...All the days ordained for me were written in your book before one of them came to be.** (Verse 16)

This powerful declaration reveals *purpose* for each individual created by God. It explains the reason for our existence. God assigns our purpose. He is who *decides* it, and we *discover* it. The word, *ordain,* is defined as follows:

To invest officially (as by the laying on of hands) with ministerial or priestly authority; to establish or order by appointment, decree, or law.[2]

What comes first, the *creation* of the product or the *purpose* of the product? It is obvious that the purpose of the product being designed or invented is determined *first*, and *then* the product is fashioned in accordance with its intended purpose. Before you were fashioned in your mother's womb, your purpose was ordained or assigned to you. When God formed you in the womb, He designed you in total *alignment* for you to live out the "days ordained" for you.

> *When God formed you in the womb, He designed you in total alignment for you to live out the "days ordained" for you!*

JEREMIAH: THE PROPHET

God spoke to Jeremiah at a very young age, revealing His purpose for his life. The account is amazing! Jeremiah learned that even before he had a chance to look at himself in the mirror, God had already seen and known him. Additionally, God revealed to Jeremiah that he had been sanctified (separated, consecrated, anointed, appointed or ordained) to do something specific with his life:

"Before I formed you in the womb I knew you, before you were born I set you apart; I appointed you as a prophet to the nations." (Jeremiah 1:5)

Here are some observations about this verse:

- God is your Creator.
- God was not surprised with your birth.
- God assigns your purpose *before* you are born.
- God decides your purpose; you discover it.
- God knows you better than you know yourself.

Imagine this conversation between God and Jeremiah. God tells Jeremiah what his purpose in life is, and Jeremiah responds to God by saying that he doesn't even know how to speak and that he is too young for the task. It reveals how shocking this experience was for this young man. Jeremiah thought he knew himself and now discovers that someone else knows much more about him than he does! *Before* he was born, God had already made "arrangements" for his entire life!

I have heard parents refer to a child as an accident or a surprise. Parents may be surprised, but it is not a surprise to God. To God, you are a work of art destined to carry out a specific purpose on earth.

If we could interview Jeremiah today and ask him what his life purpose is, he would answer: "My life purpose is to be a prophet to the nations."

Please note that the scope of his ministry was broad, "to the nations." Jeremiah prophesied to a total of ten nations. By reading the book of Jeremiah you will discover that he addressed the following nations: Judah, Egypt, Philistia, Moab, Ammon, Edom, Damascus (Syria), Arabia, Elam and Babylon. In contrast, there were other prophets whose geographical area of ministry wasn't as wide ranging. For instance, the ministry of the prophet Joel was confined to the Southern Kingdom of Judah, while Hosea only prophesied to the Northern Kingdom of Israel. A deeper study of the lives and ministries of these characters reveals how unique each one of them was. They each lived in different times, and the content and the method of delivering their message was very diverse. It is important to note these differences because even when our purpose is similar to someone else's, there always will be notable differences that make us unique.

PAUL: THE APOSTLE

The life of the Apostle Paul is of great interest to most preachers. The account of his life before becoming a Christian, his conversion to Christianity, and his life after his great encounter with Christ is fascinating! Paul is a man of great passion, great accomplishments in the spreading of the Gospel, which came with great suffering.

People would plot to kill Paul (Acts 23:12), and they would make oaths not to taste or drink anything until they achieved their objective! Often, he was chased from one city to another. Multitudes would turn against him, stone him and leave him for dead. His friends would come to his aid, and the next day he would be preaching the Gospel in the same corner of that city! It is hard to believe that just a few years earlier he was the one chasing, mistreating, harassing, terrorizing and imprisoning Christians everywhere.

I have always wondered the following about Paul: What kept him going? What was the fuel that energized him? What caused this great change? What motivated him? Why did he love Christ much more than his own life? I have come to the conclusion that *knowing his purpose* was the fuel that energized him.

Following Paul's great encounter with Christ, he was blinded for three days and didn't eat or drink anything. God instructed a disciple named Ananias to go pray for Paul and gave him the address of the house of the person whom Paul was staying with (Acts 9:1-19). Initially, Ananias was reluctant to follow this instruction because everyone in the region knew the reputation Paul had created for himself as a fierce persecutor of the Christians. Nevertheless, God revealed to Ananias His purpose for the life of the Apostle Paul: "Go! This man is my chosen instrument to carry my name before the Gentiles and their kings and before the people of Israel." (Acts 9:15)

If we were to interview the Apostle Paul today and ask him what his life purpose is, his answer would be very clear: "My life purpose is to take God's name to gentiles, kings and the Jews."

God assigns a specific task to each individual, at a particular time, for a special purpose. Every person is born with everything they need to fulfill their God-given purpose.

CHAPTER 22

THE ANOINTING AND PURPOSE

The anointing and our life purpose are closely related. The clearer the understanding regarding your purpose, the greater the anointing will flow within you.

My experience has been that the term *anointing* is not understood easily. Its meaning has been diluted and downgraded. It's often reduced to not much more than feelings and emotions. This term is used so loosely nowadays that it contributes to the misunderstanding and confusion about its intended meaning.

Let's take an in-depth biblical look at the meaning of anointing, how the anointing oil was made, how the act of anointing was performed, and on whom and on what it was used.

THE INGREDIENTS

God revealed the ingredients for this uncommon oil to Moses:

Moreover, the LORD spoke to Moses, saying, "Take also for

yourself the finest of spices: of flowing myrrh five hundred shekels, and of fragrant cinnamon half as much, two hundred and fifty, and of fragrant cane two hundred and fifty, and of cassia five hundred, according to the shekel of the sanctuary, and of olive oil a hin. And you shall make of these holy anointing oil, a perfume mixture, the work of a perfumer; it shall be a holy anointing oil." (Exodus 30:22-25)

THE USE

The following verses disclose the purpose of this holy anointing oil.

1. TO ANOINT THINGS

In the following verses, we can observe the different objects that God ordained to be anointed:

"Then use it to anoint the Tent of Meeting, the ark of the Testimony, the table and all its articles, the lamp stand and its accessories, the altar of incense, the altar of burnt offering and all its utensils, and the basin with its stand. You shall consecrate them so they will be most holy, and whatever touches them will be holy." (Exodus 30:26-29)

2. TO ANOINT PERSONS

God established that people in special positions of authority be anointed:

"Anoint Aaron and his sons and consecrate them so they may serve me as priests." (Exodus 30:30)

Therefore, we learn that the holy anointing oil was used to anoint and consecrate:

- The tent and all its utensils.
- Those who were appointed by God to serve as priests.

There are two words that are usually mentioned together: *anoint*

115

and *consecrate*. These are the Hebrew meanings of the term *anoint:*

- **Mashach** (maw-shakh) "This is a primitive root; to rub with oil, i.e. to anoint; by implication, to consecrate; also to paint." [1]
- **Mashiyach** (maw-shee'-akh) "Anointed; usually a consecrated person (as a king, priest, or saint); specifically, the Messiah." [2]

Here is the Hebrew meaning for the term *consecrate:*

- **Qadash** (kaw-dash) "Appoint, bid, consecrate, dedicate, hallow, (be, keep) holy, keep, prepare, proclaim, purify, sanctify, wholly." [3]

Anyone and anything that God chooses to be dedicated to serve Him in any capacity must be *anointed* and *consecrated* for a specific purpose. Based on the information above about anointing and consecrating, I define these two terms as follows:

Anoint: A ceremonial process whereby holy anointing oil is applied (rubbed) either to things or persons whom God chooses to consecrate (appoint, dedicate, set apart, ordain) for a specific purpose.

Consecrate: To set apart, to appoint, to dedicate, to devote or to ordain something or someone for a specific purpose through an anointing ceremony.

3. TO ANOINT KINGS

In addition to anointing the tent and its furniture along with the priests who were consecrated to serve God, kings and priests were also anointed.

Anointing a king was equivalent to crowning him. In fact, in Israel a crown wasn't required. David was anointed as king by the prophet Samuel, and initially he didn't receive a crown:

> Then Samuel took the horn of oil and anointed him in the midst of his brothers; and the Spirit of the LORD came mightily upon David from that day forward. And Samuel arose and went to Ramah. (1 Samuel 16:13)

4. TO ANOINT PROPHETS

Prophets were also referred to as anointed:

> Do not touch My anointed ones, and do My prophets no harm. (Psalm 105:15)

THE ANOINTING OF JESUS

The passage found in Luke 4:18-19 clearly reveals the relationship between *anointing* and *purpose*. On the Sabbath day, Jesus entered a synagogue and the book of Isaiah was given to Him to read. Note carefully what he read:

> The Spirit of the Lord is on me, because he has anointed me to preach good news to the poor. He has sent me to proclaim freedom for the prisoners and recovery of sight for the blind, to release the oppressed, to proclaim the year of the Lord's favor. (Luke 4:18-19)

Jesus was not anointed because the Spirit of the Lord was upon Him. But rather, the Spirit of the Lord was upon Jesus because He had been anointed.

Jesus declares that the Spirit of the Lord is upon Him and then explains *why*. Carefully notice his explanation: "...because He [the Lord] *has* anointed me to..."

Before Jesus was sent to us, He *had* already been *anointed* and *consecrated* to perform everything he mentioned in those verses. Here is the great revelation: Jesus was not anointed *because* the Spirit of the Lord was upon Him. Rather, the Spirit of the

Lord was upon Jesus because He *had been anointed.*

The apostle Paul also explains this connection.

> Now it is God who makes both us and you stand firm in Christ. *He anointed us,* set his seal of ownership on us, *and put his Spirit in our hearts* as a deposit, guaranteeing what is to come. (II Corinthians 1:21-22 emphasis added.)

Paul the Apostle states clearly that God first anointed us then put His Spirit in us. The same that was true for David, Jeremiah, Moses, Nehemiah and Paul is true for you and me. Before we were born, God *anointed* us for a specific purpose. The question that begs an answer is... what have you been anointed for? You are not anointed because the Spirit of the Lord is in you — the Spirit of the Lord is in you because you have been anointed to do a specific task. When you know what that task is, the anointing will become available to you in ways you haven't experienced before. The Holy Spirit, who in essence is the presence of God, will give you the power that will enable you to live out the purpose for which you *have been anointed.*

SIX FACTS ABOUT ANOINTING AND PURPOSE

1. God *has anointed* you for a specific purpose.
2. The anointing is *directly related* to your purpose.
3. Discovering your life purpose is *knowing* what you *have been anointed* to do.
4. To walk in His anointing, you must *know* what He has anointed you for.
5. The greater your *understanding* about your purpose, the greater the *anointing* will flow within you.
6. Understanding this connection should lead you to focus on *discovering* your life purpose.

You are now equipped with a greater knowledge and understanding about the relationship between anointing and purpose. Like Jesus, when you discover your life purpose you will be able to complete the following statement:

"The Spirit of the Lord is upon me, because the Lord has anointed me to: _____."

Moses would say:

"The Spirit of the Lord is upon me because He has anointed me to… *be a liberator.*"

Jeremiah would say:

"The Spirit of the Lord is upon me, because He has anointed me to… *prophesy to the nations.*"

I remind myself often:

The Spirit of the Lord in upon me because He has anointed me to… *empower people to discover their life purpose and to unlock God's greatness that resides inside them.*

CHAPTER 23

LIFE'S PURPOSE
DEFINITION AND SOURCE

In this chapter, we will focus our attention on the definition and the source of our life purpose.

PURPOSE DEFINED

Purpose has become a very popular word in the last several years. One of the meanings of purpose is: "The reason for which something exists or is done, made, used, etc."[1]

As it relates to one's life purpose, I would like to provide the following definition: *Purpose is the intention and the reason for which we have been designed and created.*

THE SOURCE OF PURPOSE

If you will embrace the idea that you, as an individual, have a purpose, embracing the theology of creation will help you greatly in your quest. These beliefs cannot be divorced; it is simply impossible.

The Creator designed and gave purpose to everything He created.

Many individuals have set out to prove that the universe and its design doesn't necessitate the existence of a supernatural being. Victor J. Stenger, an emeritus professor of physics and astronomy at the University of Hawaii, writes the following:

> The scenario I have presented is consistent with all scientific observations and is based on scientific theories that are well tested. It is proposed with the modest purpose of providing a counter-example that serves to refute any assertion that the universe and its laws, as revealed by scientific data, cannot be explained without introducing an external, supernatural creator.[2]

On the other hand, there are those for whom evidence of design in our world is very clear. John F. Haught is a distinguished professor of theology at Georgetown University and director of the Georgetown Center for the Study of Science and Religion. Addressing the evidence of design in our world, he writes:

> ...the evidence of design is so ubiquitous that scientists who wish to deny its implications have had to cope with its presence...they have turned the original argument in its head. Rather than accepting that we are here because of a deliberate supernatural design, they claim that the universe simply must be this way because we are here; had the universe been otherwise, we would not be here to observe ourselves, and that is that. This is generally called the weak anthropic principle.[3]

Think about the purpose of the sun. It is the star of our solar system and directly, or indirectly, supports almost all life on earth. The sun drives the earth's climate and weather. The earth, other planets and matter orbit the sun. In order for it to accomplish its purpose, it had to be placed exactly where it is.

Someone had to design our galaxy, create every planet and star in it, and *assign* individual functions for each one so that life would be possible on earth. What a magnificent task! Someone needs to receive credit for doing it. The idea that this could randomly happen or evolve overtime requires more faith than believing that someone designed it. As we observe other areas of creation, design and purpose are evident in each of them.

This fact is obvious when we look at nature. The Creator's blueprint is seen clearly in the most miniscule facets of creation as well as in the most complex ones. I was watching one of the educational TV channels one evening and it was broadcasting one of those nature shows. They showed how journalists travel to the most remote places around the globe to capture nature at its best. At one point, they were deep into the forest of an African jungle. They explained how every insect and plant played such a vital role for the overall health of the forest. It included the micro-insects as well as the 450-pound gorillas, and all the plants and animals in-between. Each one of them carried out their purpose, and as they did, they assisted one another in fulfilling theirs. The complexity of the design is astonishing! Individually, each one of them was a building block of the entire forest.

The Creator's blueprint is seen clearly in the most miniscule facets of creation as well as in the most complex ones.

Pastor Robert Morris emphasizes that God is a God of purpose and that He created everything with purpose:

> God is a *"purpose-full"* God. He is not a "purposeless" God! He didn't create everything without purpose. Every animal, every plant, every tree, every person—including you!—every single one of God's creations has been created for a purpose. The Bible says God formed you in your mother's womb—and when He formed you, He had a purpose in mind.[4]

God is the Creator of all living creatures and the majestic universe we have come to know. We are His product, and He doesn't create anything purposeless!

CHAPTER 24

PURPOSE IS ASSIGNED
BEFORE BIRTH

God assigned your purpose before you were born.

Before God created the product (you and me), He created the purpose for the product.

God is the Creator who gives purpose and meaning to His creation and He delights in it. You have already been given, or assigned, your purpose. It's only a matter of discovering it so that you can live it out!

Accepting the theology of creation makes it easy to identify who your creator is. *Knowing* your Creator enables you to discover the reason why He created you. The Psalmist David wrote:

> Your eyes saw my unformed body. All the days ordained for me were written in your book before one of them came to be. (Psalm 139:15-16)

There is a lot of depth in the words declared in this verse. David had come to know that his life *had* been *designed* and *ordained* by God, even before he was formed in his mother's womb. This not only speaks about the time or season in which one is born, but it also includes one's purpose in life.

Our mission in life should be to discover our purpose and then live it out the rest of our days.

God saw his *unformed body* before he was born. Not only did God see it, but He also wrote in "the book" the days that were *ordained* or *purposed* for him, even though he hadn't yet lived even one of them. This is what I refer to as the *human manufacturing plant* where the Designer stamps His product with individual and unique purpose.

Addressing this topic, Robert Morris provides the following insight:

> When God speaks, His purposes are going to come to pass. Why is this so exciting? Because *God has spoken over you!* God spoke His purpose over your life when He created you! And the words God has spoken over your life will not return void. They will accomplish the thing that He sent them to do.[1]

Malphurs adds:

> Everyone has a design from God, and everyone's design is unique...God is the author and source of our makeup long before we're born into this world.[2]

Our mission in life should be to discover our purpose and then live it out the rest of our days. In so doing, not only will it affect and change us, but it will also allow us to bless others and leave our imprint in this world.

CHAPTER 25

PURPOSE IS BOTH
TEMPORAL AND ETERNAL

Purpose is temporal and eternal.

When properly identified we discover that purpose affects both the temporal and the eternal. It has its time and place in both spheres.

Throughout the history of humankind, we have been blessed with talented and gifted scientists, physicists, doctors, mathematicians, biologists, philosophers, thinkers and inventors who have left their imprint on the world.

Besides being one of the founding fathers of the United States, Benjamin Franklin was an inventor and scientist. He played a vital role in the history of physics with his theories regarding electricity and his experiments with lightning. This sparked a great interest in other physicists who paved the way for modern electricity.

The ohm (symbol: Ω), which is the unit of electrical resistance, was named after Georg Simon Ohm,[1] a German physicist. The unit of electrical potential (volt) was named after Alessandro Volta,[2] an Italian physicist. Volta is known for the development of the electric battery in 1800. Andre-Marie Ampere is another French physicist who is credited with the discovery of electromagnetism. The unit of electric current (ampere) is named after him.[3] Diseases and their cures are named after those who discovered them. Dr. Alois Alzheimer identified the first case of what is known as Alzheimer's disease (AD) in the beginning of the 20th century.[4]

Henry Ford lived from 1863 to 1947. His family wanted to keep him in the farming business, but he had no desire to work the fields. After his mother died in 1876, nothing would keep him on the family farm, which his father expected him to eventually take over. He was intrigued with mechanics since early in his life. He built a reputation for repairing clocks for his friends and neighbors. Ford left his home in 1879 and became an apprentice machinist. Later, he worked on steam machines. In 1891, he became an engineer and soon was promoted to chief engineer. By then he had a lot of experience with gasoline engines, and in 1896, he introduced his first self-propelled automobile, named the Quadricycle. In 1903, he incorporated the Ford Motor Company along with other investors. In 1908, he introduced the Model T, and this car became an immediate success. He is credited with the invention of the assembly line that allowed for mass production of vehicles. The price of the car was fair, and the price actually came down every year. This allowed more people the ability to own a car.[5]

Think about the automobile, the locomotive, the plane, electricity and medicine. The world wouldn't be the way we know and experience it if it weren't for these gifted individuals. We are grateful to them for improving the lives of billions of people around the world. They were definitely sent to us in the right time and era. The need for solutions to the problems faced in their time made way for their abilities and talents to flourish. They touched people with their inventions then and continue to benefit us today.

All these great individuals were created (designed, fashioned) with abilities, gifts, talents and interests in the particular fields that came so naturally to them. Their makeup was created on purpose. It is said that by age ten Albert Einstein was wondering how fast light travels. Not every person is captivated by such concerns, especially at that young age! Others were consumed by ideas such as flying and navigating the oceans.

Tragedy occurs when we live only with a temporal view of life.

Some of these great men and women were discouraged from pursuing their ideas, dreams and visions. However, they stayed the course, paid the price required and made the world a better place. These individuals are gifts to this world. The Bible declares:

> Every good and perfect gift is from above, coming down from the Father of the heavenly lights, who does not change like shifting shadows. (James 1:17)

Regardless of our contribution to humanity, tragedy occurs when we live only with a temporal view of life. Our lives transcend the temporal and the natural. Life escapes us like water through our hands. Our meager time on earth doesn't compare to our eternity.

> For what shall it profit a man, if he shall gain the whole world, and lose his own soul? (Mark 8:36 KJV)

Your life purpose will not only affect people in the present and temporal, but it will also affect their eternity. God is an eternal being. He is not only concerned about our current life, but even more with our life in eternity. As humans, we are *eternal* beings living in *temporal* bodies. Our purpose will always influence both spheres.

One might ask, "But how can I, being an auto mechanic, have an impact on someone's eternity?" Your profession may not affect your clients' eternity, but your purpose does. Keep in mind that your occupation doesn't define your life purpose (see page 86).

ENCOUNTER WITH PURPOSE

PART 6

SEEING
THE
BIG PICTURE

"God's visions always have an eternal element. His individual vision for your life is a small part of a plan He envisioned and put in motion long before you or I came on the scene."[1]

— Andy Stanley

SEEING THE BIG PICTURE

The objective of this section is to present purpose in its highest and truest sense.

I will use corporations as an illustration. Typically, they are formed for a specific objective. Normally, they seek to establish themselves as the leading provider of a particular product or service. They work hard to perfect what they offer. They set goals and then devise plans and strategies to accomplish them. Big marketing campaigns are conducted, and different advertising strategies are implemented.

All is done in an effort to accomplish their goals and fulfill the company's purpose. Various departments are set up and personnel are hired to market and sell their products and services. A great sales force is necessary to sell their products because no matter how good their product or service may be, if people don't know about it they won't be interested.

There are great salespersons out there, and they absolutely love what they do for a living. They work hard to achieve high levels of production, and it gives them great satisfaction. They have been highly educated and trained to perform their individual function in the corporation.

Different titles and responsibilities are assigned to individuals. The *individual* function each person performs is directly connected to the *company's* purpose. In fact, it contributes toward the overall objective of the corporation.

When individuals align themselves to the company's vision, they become more successful. When they refuse or are unwilling to align themselves with the company's vision, these employees experience frustration, lack of production, low morale, and often the exit door.

Each individual working for the company performs a unique task.

They don't choose it; it is normally assigned to them. Whether their assignment is to be the CEO, CFO, sales manager or a sales representative, by carrying out their assigned responsibilities, they are actually furthering the purpose and objectives of the organization. One can say that it is not really *their* assignment but the company's. Soon you will see how all of this ties in with your life purpose *and* God's incomparable plan for humanity.

CHAPTER 26

THE BIG PICTURE
REVEALED

To those who lack a solid Biblical understanding about life's purpose, it is merely a goal or a desire of some sort. This explains why for many people purpose is simply the pursuit of happiness, joy or success. This is a very shallow view regarding such a significant aspect of life.

Our purpose is part of God's plan, both here on earth and for eternity. It touches our circle of influence, no matter how small or broad it may be, and it affects both the now and the eternal.

What an awesome thought! I get to participate and collaborate toward the fulfillment of the greatest, the biggest, the most lasting and the most rewarding plan ever designed in the history of humanity and beyond! It behooves me to know what this plan is.

THE PLAN REVEALED

God revealed His plan to the Apostle Paul, and He laid it out this way:

> Having made known to us the mystery of His will, according to His good pleasure which He purposed in Himself, that in the dispensation of the fullness of times He might gather together in one all things in Christ, both which are in heaven, and which are on earth; even in Him. (Ephesians 1:9-10 NKJV)

Here is God's plan and design revealed to us. "In the fullness of times" refers to the time God has assigned for the planet earth to exist. When the world ends, eternity begins. God's plan, beyond that, is to bring or unite, both the *physical* (seen) and the *spiritual* (unseen) worlds, and to *merge* them into one, in Christ.

Our purpose is part of God's plan, both here on earth and for eternity.

To gain a broader understanding of these verses let's turn to a Bible commentary by Albert Barnes. He provides the following explanation:

> **The fullness of times** … The period referred to here is that when all things shall be gathered together in the Redeemer at the winding up of human affairs, or the consummation of all things …The plan stretched from before "the foundation of the world" to the period when all times should be completed; and of course all the events occurring in that intermediate period were embraced in the plan.[1]

Another great Bible commentary on this topic is the Jamieson, Fausset, and Brown Commentary. They explain the concept of "gathering together in one" as follows:

> **Gather together in one** … The good pleasure which He purposed was to sum up all things in Christ. God sums up the whole creation

in Christ, the Head of angels, with whom He is linked by His invisible nature; and of men, with whom He is linked by His humanity; of Jews and Gentiles; of the living and the dead (Eph. 3:15); of animate and inanimate creation.[2]

Barnes continues his explanation of these verses by saying:

All things ... All "things" are placed under Christ, and the design of God is to restore harmony in the universe. Sin has produced disorder not only in "mind," but in "matter." The world is disarranged. The effects of transgression are seen everywhere; and the object of the plan of redemption is to put things on their pristine footing, and restore them as they were at first. Everything is, therefore, put under the Lord Jesus, and all things are to be brought under his control, so as to constitute one vast harmonious empire ... In accordance with this view the heavenly inhabitants, the angels as well as the redeemed, are uniformly represented as uniting in the same worship, and as acknowledging the Redeemer as their common head and king.

Both which are in heaven ... The object of the plan of salvation is to produce a harmony between them and the redeemed on earth, or to produce out of all, one great and united Kingdom.

And which are on earth ... The object is to bring them into harmony with the inhabitants of heaven. This is the great object proposed by the plan of salvation. It is to found one glorious and eternal kingdom that shall comprehend all holy beings on earth and all in heaven. There is now discord and disunion. Man is separated from God, and from all holy beings. Between him and every holy being there is by nature discord and alienation. Unrenewed man has no sympathy with the feelings and work of the angels; no love for their employment; no desire to be associated with them. Nothing can be more unlike than the customs, feelings, laws, and habits which prevail on earth, from those which prevail in heaven. But the object of the plan of salvation is to restore harmony to those alienated communities, and produce eternal concord and love. Hence, we learn: *This is the greatest and most important enterprise on earth.* It should engage every heart, and enlist the powers of every soul. It should be the earnest desire of all to swell the numbers of those who shall constitute this united and ever-glorious kingdom, and to bring as many as possible of the human race into union with the holy inhabitants of the other world.[3] (Emphasis added)

What an awesome picture! Understanding God's plan helps me *see* the big picture. When I understand and see the broader picture, it allows me to see how *my purpose* will always be aligned to *His* ultimate and eternal plan.

I am part of the biggest and greatest plan ever devised on earth and beyond! Everyone has an agenda. Individuals, families and corporations do. Someone is assisting them in carrying out their plans. Whose agenda are you advancing?

I am so glad to be part of something so much bigger than me, bigger than temporal life itself. Many people are a big part of something small. They are very visible and receive all the credit. I love the idea of being part of something bigger than life. My contribution is a drop in a bucket. However, this doesn't make it any less significant. When I operate in my purpose I am advancing heaven's agenda, and I am the happiest and the most fulfilled individual. I would rather be a small part of something great than a great part of something small.

> *When you look into the cross, you can see God's supreme purpose, and in His purpose, you find yours.*

God's plan and purpose is unparalleled. When you look into the cross, you can see God's supreme purpose, and in *His* purpose, you find yours.

CHAPTER 27

YOUR PURPOSE OR
HIS PURPOSE FOR YOU?

Is not really your purpose but *His* purpose for you.

When you work for a corporation, you cannot dictate your own agenda or purpose. Whatever the tasks and responsibilities are, they will always represent the company's purpose. In everything you do, the company's best interest is first.

God didn't devise His plan yesterday. When He created you, He designed and equipped you with all the tools you will ever need to make your contribution toward His supreme plan. However, the fact that you are equipped with the tools doesn't mean you automatically know what they are, and that you can use them to their maximum capacity.

There is greatness in each one of us that often takes a long time for us to discover. In fact, sometimes we don't see it until someone else points it out to us. The maximum growth in every area of life is experienced when we properly identify God's purpose for us. It becomes your main focus — your obsession! You breathe it, speak it, and share it.

Since I discovered God's purpose for my life, I see purpose and greatness in each person. I also see a sign on their forehead that reads, "Please help me discover my purpose!" I talk about this on a daily basis with people I know and those whom I meet for the first time.

> *The maximum growth in every area of life is experienced when we properly identify God's purpose for us.*

When I see the big picture and understand God's awesome plan, I start seeking purpose with a divine perspective! I start asking the question, what is God's purpose for me? How do I contribute to His plan? I come to the understanding that my personal design and life experiences have equipped me to further His agenda.

Seeing your life purpose as *His* purpose for you is a small shift in perspective but it can have a profound effect as you pursue it.

CHAPTER 28

HAVE YOU REALLY DISCOVERED IT?

How do you know if you really have discovered your life purpose?

Most things in life have a standard by which they are measured, judged or evaluated. A standard is something set as a rule or measure.

When it comes to our life purpose, we can evaluate whether or not we have properly identified it by a standard. That standard is God's supreme plan revealed in Ephesians 1:9-10 (see page 135).

One sign or *confirmation* that you have properly identified your purpose is that it always affects people's present and their eternity, whether it is directly or indirectly.

When she was a teenager, Florence Nightingale felt a calling to follow the will of God by serving others. She felt that the way to fulfill this divine commission (purpose) was to become a nurse, but at that time, that profession was neither respected nor attractive. Her wealthy family opposed the idea. However, despite this obstacle, she received the education and training in this profesion.[1] She felt stifled by the vanities and social expectations, and felt the need to do something for those who were sick and lacked attention and basic care. Despite having opportunities to marry, she never did. Her legacy is powerful. Florence is remembered as a pioneer in nursing and a reformer of the methods of hygiene in hospitals.[2] By knowing her purpose, she received training in a profession that would help her express it. Her profession didn't define her purpose. It was a platform, however, that allowed her to exercise it. She ministered God's love as she nurtured back to health those who were sick or injured in battle.

If God's intention was for your purpose to touch only the natural and the temporal, He wouldn't have put eternity in you.

If what you think your purpose is fails to provide, directly or indirectly, any *eternal value* to others, then what you have discovered is your occupation, or your talents and abilities, not your life purpose.

If God's intention was for your purpose to touch only the natural and the temporal, He wouldn't have put eternity in you. You are an eternal being. Your natural death is the gateway to perpetuity.

So the best manner for us to evaluate our purpose is to see if it aligns properly with God's supreme plan.

CHAPTER 29

YOU AND GOD'S SUPREME PLAN

What an honor to learn that you and I get to participate and contribute in the fulfillment of God's supreme purpose! I don't have to, if I choose not to. You don't have to do it, if you choose not to. It would be wrong for us to think that to fulfill His purpose He needs us more than we need Him, or that He won't accomplish it without our contribution.

God makes known His great plan for all humankind and our response doesn't invalidate His stated objective.

There is an account in Luke 14:16 where an invitation to a party was sent out to some individuals who seemed to be well off financially. When all was ready for the banquet, they all began to excuse themselves, citing different reasons for not attending. I think one may have been a Texan because he had just bought some land and had to take care of it! Someone else had just gotten married and was off to his honeymoon. When the news was given to the host, he gave orders to his workers to go into the street corners, highways and byways and to invite as many as would accept his invitation. His party was ready and one way or another it was going to take place. He had put a lot into his plan, and he was going forward with it.

God has revealed His plan to us. It is the heartbeat of God to bring both the physical and the spiritual worlds together in Christ! He has included you and me in His plan. Are you in it? Can He count on you? His desire is for you to be part of His team. However, if you refuse to play, it doesn't mean He will lose the game. It does mean that you could lose your opportunity to score some points on His behalf!

> *Men and women who respond to His call always advance God's agenda.*

Men and women who respond to His call always advance God's agenda. This is the method He has chosen since He created the world and then rested.

When God wanted to raise a nation, He called Abraham who had no children and was very old (Genesis 12:1). To bring the people out of Egypt He called Moses (Exodus 3 and 4). To rebuild the city of Jerusalem He used Nehemiah and Zerubbabel (books of Ezra and Nehemiah). To bring salvation to this world He sent His son, Jesus, who was born of the Virgin Mary (Mathew 1:18). To spread His message of salvation He has chosen to use ordinary people, like you and I.

When the first king was established in Israel, God chose Saul to lead this new office (1 Samuel 10:1). After a few years, Saul decided to lead his own way and to ignore God's instructions. God didn't abolish the newly established form of government; He removed Saul from the office and placed David in his position (1 Samuel 16:13).

Our life purpose is linked directly to our Creator and His divine plan to bring all things together in Christ, the visible and the invisible. This is huge! It is bigger than anyone's agenda or ingenious idea. This *is* the *Big Picture!* Can you see it? Can you believe that you are part of it? Can you see yourself in it?

The next section focuses on discovering where you fit in this gigantic picture.

PART 7

DISCOVERING
YOUR
LIFE PURPOSE

"You were tailor-made, carefully crafted, minutely detailed for a selected divine agenda."[1]

— Andy Stanley

DISCOVERING YOUR LIFE PURPOSE

On a certain occasion, I dislocated one of my ankles and I was referred to a massage therapist who treats this type of injury. I never knew that my feet and toes could swell so much. My big toe was about three times its normal size, and of course, the pain was unbearable! I couldn't set any part of my foot on the floor. The pain was excruciating. It would hurt even when I walked on crutches.

The therapist looked at my enlarged foot and said that I would be able to put my foot on the floor after he was done. He also added that he would help me on one condition—if I *loaned* him my foot. I knew what this meant, and I agreed. It was painful to say the least! It almost hurts me again just to remember. After about an hour of preparation and treatment, the pain was reduced by about 90 percent and I was able to set my foot lightly on the floor, just like he had said. Three days later, I was walking fine. It was quite an intense experience!

The information presented in this section will be very intense, and it will benefit you the most if you can dedicate the quality time needed. Prepare well for it mentally and emotionally. Don't rush through it. If you can set a better time for it, please do so.

Get a pen and a clear mind to go through all the exercises and answer all the questions. Most of these questions will require your total focus and proper attitude.

This process won't hurt nearly as much as my ankle experience—at least that is not my intention. But it does require that you *lend* yourself totally to the pursuit of discovering your purpose.

CHAPTER 30

DIFFERENT WAYS TO DISCOVER IT

Is there a formula for discovering our life purpose?

It would be rather simple and mechanical if there was a formula. However, I think it would also violate the principle of individuality, which is essential in this subject matter.

Rather than seeking for a formula as a means to discover it, I would like you to remain completely open to different ways you may encounter purpose. Let's look at five possible ways to discover it.

1. REVELATION THROUGH INFORMATION

One method, and probably the most common one, to discover your life purpose is through the pursuit of information about this topic.

The information must be accurate and biblically sound. When properly received and internalized, it awakens your purpose.

This method can be viewed as information that causes a revelation—it's not just head knowledge. Despite good intentions, taking scriptural information out of context to satisfy this quest only creates confusion, frustration and more questions, not answers.

> *Despite good intentions, taking scriptural information out of context to satisfy this quest only creates confusion, frustration and more questions, not answers.*

Using this method, I have coached individuals to discover their life purpose. The information has enthused individuals and provoked a strong determination to discover it. After removing layers of misconceptions and wrong information, purpose has looked them in their eyes.

2. INDIRECT REVELATION

Indirect revelation is when God reveals a person's life purpose through someone else.

This was the case with the Apostle Paul, formerly known as Saul. Initially, God didn't reveal His purpose directly to Paul. Instead, God instructed Paul to go to the city (Damascus) and that there he would be told what he must do (Acts 9:6). Then, the Lord spoke to a man named Ananias, gave him the physical address where Paul was staying in Damascus, and commanded him to go see Paul. Ananias wasn't very enthusiastic about this task because he knew Paul's bad reputation among his Christian peers. It is at this point that God revealed Paul's life purpose to Ananias:

> But the Lord said to Ananias, "Go! This man is my chosen instrument to carry my name before the Gentiles and their kings and before the people of Israel." (Acts 9:15)

This marked a new beginning in the life of this great Apostle and undoubtedly, God revealed many other things directly to him.

When God was to make David the king of Israel, He didn't reveal it directly to David. God commanded the Prophet Samuel to fill his horn with oil and to head out to Bethlehem to anoint one of Jesse's sons as king (I Samuel 16:1-13). Samuel met with Jesse and had him bring all his sons. When Eliab came, probably the biggest and oldest son, Samuel thought to himself that he was looking at the next king of Israel. He was wrong!

> But the LORD said to Samuel, "Do not consider his appearance or his height, for I have rejected him. The LORD does not look at the things man looks at. Man looks at the outward appearance, but the LORD looks at the heart." (1 Sam 16:7)

Samuel called for the next son, and the next one, until seven of them had stood in front of Samuel, but God didn't choose any of them. Samuel asked Jesse if he had another son. Jesse was reluctant to bring David because he was the youngest and just a little shepherd boy. Samuel insisted.

> So he sent and had him brought in. He was ruddy, with a fine appearance and handsome features. Then the LORD said, "Rise and anoint him; he is the one." So Samuel took the horn of oil and anointed him in the presence of his brothers, and from that day on the Spirit of the LORD came upon David in power. Samuel then went to Ramah. (1 Sam 16:12-13)

In this example, David's life purpose is revealed to him indirectly through the Prophet Samuel.

3. DIRECT REVELATION

Another way of discovering one's purpose is by direct revelation from God.

Moses had the famous encounter with God in the burning bush.

God revealed His purpose to Moses directly ... to *deliver* the children of Israel out of the oppression of the Egyptians to a land that flowed with milk and honey (Exodus 3).

Mary, the mother of Jesus, received a visitation from the angel Gabriel, and her purpose was revealed to her (Luke 1:26-38). Jeremiah received a direct revelation from the Lord about his life purpose (Jeremiah 1:5).

You are probably wondering if these experiences could happen in the 21st century. The answer is yes. My daughter Gianna also discovered her purpose by direct revelation at age six. It happened while I had embarked in this holy journey to discover my own life purpose. One day, as we were all gathered in our living room, I asked her if she knew what her purpose was. She immediately responded: "To be a prophetess, to deliver Bibles around the world and to tell others about God." Her answer came without any hesitation or effort. Obviously, we were all in awe. The next evening as we were having dinner, I asked her how she knew that was her life purpose. She explained to me what happened on the night she received this direct revelation. This is her account:

> Daddy, when I was in my bedroom last night, I heard the voice of Jesus that came from the closet. His voice was like when He spoke to His disciples. (As if she had been there and actually heard the tone of His voice.) And He said, "By tomorrow afternoon you will know your purpose in life." But, Daddy, He didn't tell me what my purpose was. He just said that I would know it by tomorrow afternoon. So when you asked me if I knew my purpose, I just blurted it out!"

Ever since this experience, Gianna continues to gain a deeper understanding about her life purpose. Her level of maturity and depth of understanding of spiritual matters is very uncommon for her age. She published her first book, *How to Live Life with Purpose and Passion*, when she was eight. At age nine, Gianna said to me that she will never forget precisely when this understanding came and even in the position she was on the carpet floor of our living room when I asked her the question.

4. REVELATION THROUGH AVAILABILITY

Isaiah the prophet is a perfect example of people who discover their life purpose through availability.

In the book of Isaiah chapter six, Isaiah had great vision about God, who revealed Isaiah's spiritually bankrupt condition and of those around him. In this vision, Isaiah's sin is purged and right after that he hears a voice saying, "Whom shall I send? And who will go for us?" His immediate response was, "Here am I. Send me!" (Isaiah 6:8). Nothing is revealed about where this person will be sent or the nature of this assignment. Isaiah doesn't feel the need to know the details about his commission; he is simply responding in obedience to a proposal. There is no direct command and it is not a personal invitation either. It is simply an act of obedience to a perceived need. He makes himself fully *available* and in turn comes face to face with his own life purpose.

The first four disciples that Jesus called into ministry received the revelation of their life purpose by making themselves *available* to a call or an invitation. Peter, Andrew, James and John were called before Jesus ever performed one miracle or healed one person. Around the time of their calling, Jesus was not widely known. They didn't follow Jesus because they *knew* the details about His invitation. Jesus didn't hold a meeting to explain all the benefits of following Him. They didn't choose to follow Jesus because they were promised health insurance coverage and two weeks' vacation after the first year of service. Here is the account of the first Apostles that Jesus called:

As Jesus was walking beside the Sea of Galilee, he saw two brothers,

Simon called Peter and his brother Andrew. They were casting a net into the lake, for they were fishermen. "Come, follow me," Jesus said, "and I will make you fishers of men." At once they left their nets and followed him. Going on from there, he saw two other brothers, James son of Zebedee and his brother John. They were in a boat with their father Zebedee, preparing their nets. Jesus called them, and immediately they left the boat and their father and followed him. (Matt 4:18-20-22)

Matthew was a tax collector when Jesus extended his call in a similar way:

As Jesus went on from there, he saw a man named Matthew sitting at the tax collector's booth. "Follow me," he told him, and Matthew got up and followed him. (Matt 9:9)

Initially, these men may have been uncertain about their response to this invitation. However, history proves that they embraced and lived out their purpose. Some of them were beheaded, and others were crucified. They were willing to lay their lives for a cause that they *knew* to be much bigger that themselves!

It may be possible that some people will discover their life purpose by making themselves available to a cause or a need. As they give themselves totally, they will experience the greatest satisfaction ever!

5. A COMBINATION OF THESE METHODS

Be open to the possibility of discovering your life purpose through a combination of the methods explained previously.

After I shared some of the information contained in this book, someone discovered her life purpose through a direct revelation from the Lord, in a dream. In the dream, she was instructed to write down what was being revealed about her life purpose. As soon as she wrote it, she woke up. She was ecstatic to finally get an answer for something she pursued for many years. I would consider this example a combination of revelation through information and direct revelation. By being exposed to the information, this person was stirred to pursue her life purpose. In the middle of this journey, she received a direct revelation!

If you had any reservations as to how you may discover your life purpose, I hope they are gone by now. God deals with each one of us in very individual ways.

Whichever way or method you experience, expect an encounter in which purpose will look straight into your eyes and say, "Thank you for diligently seeking me. I have been waiting for you. Now let's go make it happen!"

CHAPTER 31

ATTITUDE AND PERSPECTIVE

Attitude determines results.

I treat this topic with much respect and reverence — I don't take it lightly at all. It has the greatest degree of importance both for God and for people. It involves the sanctity of life and the reason for our own existence. As you pursue the discovery of your purpose, I recommend that you approach it with much care and respect also.

In addition to this reverential attitude, I suggest you express to God your desire for discovering your purpose and ask for His guidance in this journey.

Getting upset or frustrated may not help you in this process. It is important to approach it properly.

While I was coaching a person very dear to me, we addressed this topic. After a few sessions, she emailed me the poem below, which I am sharing with her permission:

Can you hear me? Hello?
I'm calling on you!
Can you tell me what it is that I'm here to do?
I need to know the truth.
Can you show me my purpose?
Thinking and not knowing it got
Me feeling like I'm worthless.
Not really living, simply existing,
Occupying space, living off the air.
Believing only in what's visually there.
Living only as far as the eye can see;
Where there's no hope, no place,
No faith, no life for me.
Are you listening? I'm calling on you.
I need to know what it is that I'm here to do.[1]

I really enjoyed this poem. I believe it embodies a great attitude and perspective about the pursuit of purpose. It also represents multitudes that are eager to discover their life purpose.

YOU FIND WHAT YOU LOOK FOR

I have learned the following principle: You find what you look for. I am not trying to be funny either!

For you to be able to find something, you must first know exactly what you are seeking. For instance, if you look for greatness in other people, you will find something in them that you can celebrate. If you look for faults, you will find many. Once you identify what you are looking for, it becomes obvious and you start seeing it everywhere.

My wife and I have been blessed with two beautiful daughters. Since we had them, I have come to know many families who have only girls also. The fact is that I already knew many of them but I didn't really *notice* it before. Since this is something very meaningful to me, I started noticing it just about everywhere! I wanted to ask moms and dads what it is like to have only girls. I started looking for them, and I am still finding them everywhere. Here is a quiz for you: Name two U.S. presidents who have no sons, only daughters. (Hint: 43rd and 44th.)

Purpose and God's greatness in people are of great interest to me. As a result, I see them everywhere. They have become more obvious, easier to understand and to share with others.

When you start focusing on your purpose, chances are that you will find it, or you may notice it *staring* at you!

CHAPTER 32

DEFINE YOUR VALUES

Two principles guide our lives: our purpose and our values.

Whether these are properly identified or not, they create the launching pad for everything we do. Purpose and values determine what we do — interests, how we do it — quality, and why you do it — motives.

The objective of this chapter is to:

- *Understand* the importance of our values.
- *Discern* how they affect all we do.
- *Define* your values.
- *Adopt* values that will launch you toward your desired destiny.

I define a *value* as something that is very important to us. Values are aspects of life we treasure. It is so important for us to have our values clearly defined.

How you react to different situations and challenges in life, and even the places you visit or choose not to, are influenced by your values. Most of the things you have done with your life so far can be traced back to your purpose and values. I see both of these as siblings.

Where you may find yourself today, financially and health wise is the result of your values. If exercising on a regular basis is one of your values, chances are you don't have serious health issues. The opposite is also true.

Life has a way of launching us in certain directions that we often dislike. The fact is that if we check our values, it shouldn't come as a surprise. A man who values faithfulness is not likely to be disloyal to his spouse. Being faithful isn't something he *has* to be but rather something he *loves* being because he has put great value on faithfulness. This value will determine whom he chooses as friends and associates. The way such a man would handle a situation where faithfulness is at risk, is basically *predetermined* – he won't even entertain the idea. If, however, he hasn't adopted faithfulness as a value, he would be more likely to yield to extramarital affairs without much resistance.

> *Where you may find yourself today, financially and health wise is the result of your values.*

Joseph was a young man in the Bible who really treasured loyalty and faithfulness. He lived by these principles and was willing to suffer false accusations, and even be thrown in jail, before being unfaithful to God and to his boss! Long before his boss' wife seduced him, he had adopted loyalty and faithfulness as treasures in his life. These values were big in him – he lived by them! Life launched him in a certain direction ... not the most desirable one, initially. He stayed true to his values and eventually rose to be the governor of Egypt, second in power after Pharaoh. His values greatly influenced the *direction* in which his life was launched.

Even if you have done a similar exercise in the past, I encourage you to engage in this one with the perspective presented in this chapter. I find it amazing how once defined, values can have a powerful effect in us.

MY CURRENT VALUES

From the chart below please circle ten values that you *currently* live by. These should be evident in your daily life.

LIST OF VALUES

Adventure	Affection	Creativity
Dance	Discipleship	Evangelism
Fame	Family	Happiness
Fitness	Friendship	Generosity
Goals	Health	Humor
Inner Harmony	Integrity	Leadership
Loyalty	Marital Faithfulness	Order
Peace	Personal Growth	Pleasure
Potential	Power	Progress
Purpose	Responsibility	Self-Respect
Self-Care	Service	Sexual Purity
Spiritual Growth	Sobriety	Sports
Truth	Wealth	Wisdom

From the list of values above, choose any additional values you would like to adopt and to live by.

_____

_____

List other values you consider very important.

_____

_____

DEFINE YOUR VALUES

Select your top five values in order of importance and define what they mean to you. For example, to you marital faithfulness may mean commitment, keeping a promise or peace of mind.

1. Value: _____

Meaning: _____

_____

2. Value: _____

Meaning: _____

_____

3. Value: _____

Meaning: _____

_____

4. Value: _____

Meaning: _____

_____

5. Value: _____

Meaning: _____

_____

Now that you have defined, and maybe adapted additional values, you are ready to move to the next step in discovering your life purpose, which is eagerly awaiting you for a meaningful encounter!

CHAPTER 33

GATHER INFORMATION

Information leads you to sources.

In this chapter we focus on gathering vital information. Following are three exercises to assist you gather data from different sources. In the first exercise, you will review fundamental information regarding purpose. Read the following statements, indicate whether you agree with them and answer the questions that follow. Preferably, finish each exercise before moving to the next.

1. PERSPECTIVE AND KNOWLEDGE ABOUT PURPOSE

☐ I am fully persuaded to discover my life purpose.
☐ I meditate frequently about what my life purpose may be.
☐ I would consider it a tragedy for me to die without discovering and fulfilling my life purpose.

My top three reasons for pursuing purpose are:

1. _____

2. _____

3. _____

When I discover my purpose, I expect to experience the following:

_____

I understand that to discover my life purpose the following efforts and attitudes are required of me:

_____

Five common beliefs about life's purpose are:

1. _____
2. _____
3. _____
4. _____
5. _____

Six dominant philosophies about life's purpose are:

1. _____
2. _____
3. _____
4. _____
5. _____
6. _____

2. OBTAINING INPUT FROM OTHERS

I mentioned earlier how we often fail to see the greatness in us until someone else points it out. There are many things we are very good at, that we just take for granted because it comes naturally to us. We don't think much of it until we see how someone else struggles with things we consider rather simple. And when we share a suggestion to make someone's life a little easier they say, "That is so simple, why didn't I think of that!" We wonder the same!

One way of getting input about yourself from others is to invite them to speak at your funeral. This is one exercise I normally ask my life-coaching clients to complete. In the subject of your e-mail write, "You are invited to my funeral" and send it to a few friends and relatives. Ask them to be honest in sharing with you what they would say at your funeral.

When seeking input from others about you, you may let them know that you are pursuing the discovery of your purpose and it means a great deal to you; what your philosophy about life's purpose is; and why you are asking them to participate. Their input can serve you as a clue in your quest. When you are seriously looking for something, you don't leave a stone unturned.

Obtaining input from others can be a double-edged sword, so be very careful! You need someone who will give an honest, unbiased opinion about you.

3.   CHILDHOOD HINTS

There is one commonly quoted proverb in the Bible that I had never been satisfied with its common interpretation and application. It is found in Proverbs 22:6 and it reads:

> Train up a child in the way he should go, Even when he is old he will not depart from it. (ESV)

The common interpretation is that "the way" refers to God's ways or laws. Now, I understand that "the way" refers to the *child's way*, or his *purpose.* This fact is further confirmed when I read the same verse in a different version of the Bible:

> Train up a boy on the opening of his way, even when he is old, he will not turn aside from it. (The Literal Translation)

The seeds of purpose may start to spring up at a surprisingly young age, as it was the experience of Samuel and Jeremiah, whose purpose was revealed early in their lives.

Parents bear a great responsibility in assisting their children in the *opening* or *discovery* of their purpose. Special attention must be given to the inclinations they demonstrate when they are young. The proper environment also must be made available for them to start developing and growing into their purpose.

Through coaching and continual conversations she hears from us, our younger daughter, Nathalia, discovered her life purpose when she was four years old. Her personality and attitude confirms to me that she is on the right path. This is her life purpose statement: "To share the love of Jesus and to make people laugh!"

This is something that just came out of her. I can testify that she lives out her purpose every day. She is very affectionate and full of joy! Her joy naturally bubbles out of her in all she does. She never goes very long without laughing at something or because of something. She is the only person I know of that can tickle herself and laugh as hard as if someone else was tickling her! When she plays soccer the faster she dribbles the ball, the harder she laughs!

> *Parents bear a great responsibility in assisting their children in the opening or discovery of their purpose.*

One day we were talking about the countries where Christians are persecuted and often killed. During our conversation, Nathalia explained, "Mom, I don't want to go to those countries where they kill Christians. I don't think that is part of my ministry!" She was four at that time.

Now let's take an introspective look. As you work on this exercise, think about your earliest possible memories as a child. What we are looking for are hints that we may trace back to our childhood. These often help to unlock questions as to why we pursue our current interests.

As you think about the following questions, be aware that they may hold some answers to your quest and may assist you in putting this puzzle together.

CHILDHOOD

What was your answer(s), when you were asked what you wanted to be when you grew up?

_____

What were you very interested in or curious about?

_____

Who did you most admire, and why?

_____

What was a dream or passion you had when you were a child?

_____

As a child, what was one place you dreamed of visiting, and why?

_____

Is there a *pattern* in things you have done, researched, participated in, volunteered for or explored as a child, a teenager, young adult, and in the present?

_____

Are there any *dots* that you can connect from your childhood to where you are in life now?

_____

_____

Fantastic! You are finished gathering vital information that you will need for the following chapter.

In this chapter you have:

- Checked your knowledge and perspectives about purpose.
- Obtained input from others.
- Looked for childhood hints.

Way to go! You are a step closer to your encounter with purpose!

CHAPTER 34

PURPOSE REVEALING QUESTIONS

Questions are keys that unlock answers.

This chapter consists of powerful questions designed to assist you to get to your core. They are a great tool to assist you in discovering the reason for your existence.

It may take you several hours, or even days, to complete this exercise, and that is okay because it provokes you to think deeply and to assess yourself honestly. Remember that we are looking for the reason for your existence, and this is not something trivial.

Purpose awaits you…are you ready? Let's do it!

I experience a great sense of fulfillment when I …

_____

_____

I experience a great sense of self-worth when I …

_____

_____

I am most excited in life when I ...

_____

I always stand for ...

_____

I never tolerate ...

_____

In the past, I have been told that I am great at ...

_____

In the past, I have excelled at ...

_____

My greatest strength is ...

_____

My main weakness is ...

_____

The traits that best describe my character are ...

_____

In the past, I have added value to others by ...

_____

If I ever reach a point in my life where money isn't an issue, I am willing to dedicate the rest of my days doing the following, without getting paid …

_____

_____

If it is was revealed to me that I only had five years to live, for me to feel that I have completed my purpose on earth, I would absolutely have to accomplish the following …

_____

_____

I would like the following inscription on my tombstone …

_____

_____

After I pass away, my family will remember me most for …

_____

_____

After I pass away, my friends and acquaintances will remember me most for …

_____

_____

At my funeral service, my pastor would say the following about me …

_____

_____

My contribution to this world is …

_____

_____

I was born to …

_____

_____

My purpose in life is to …

_____

_____

This exercise is very powerful, and I am confident that it has yielded a great deal of information about your purpose. It points you in the correct direction, which can lead you directly into your purpose.

After you have completed this exercise, it is a good idea to go back after a couple of days and review your answers. You might discover that your answers may become more clear to you as you review them a second or even a third time.

Equipped with the information you have acquired about your values and your purpose, you are now ready to write your life purpose statement.

CHAPTER 35

WRITE YOUR LIFE PURPOSE STATEMENT

There are some things to keep in mind when you work on your life purpose statement:

- Initially, your purpose statement may be very long.
- Don't expect to get it exactly right the very first time.
- It may take some time for you to "fine-tune" your statement.
- Your purpose statement declares *what* your purpose is.
- Don't include *how* you will live out your purpose in the statement.

My initial statement was a few paragraphs long, and I kept trying to condense it. It took me a few months to refine it!

As your newly discovered life purpose becomes more clear, your statement will become shorter and more precise. It also will start to feel as if it *fits* you better.

Bob Buford, who believes that the second half of your life can be better than the first, writes:

> Developing a *personal* mission statement makes a lot of sense, especially for the second-halfers ... You will not get very far in your second half without knowing your life mission. Can yours be stated in a sentence or two?[1]

> My life mission is: To transform the latent energy in American Christianity into active energy. This is what I do; it is how I want my life to count. It releases me to be myself — to use gifts that are already there. I do not have to become something that feels uncomfortable or strange. If your own mission statement fit you as well, it will be the right one for you. If it forces you into something that does not fit, it will be someone else's mission.[2]

It is possible that for a moment, you feel very sure about it and at other times, you will question it. You will gain more confidence about your purpose as it becomes more real and clear to you. It is similar to learning to ride a bike — the more you engage in it, the faster you develop the balance needed, and you become more confident as the fear of falling fades away.

As the days and weeks go by, you will feel more comfortable and confident about your newly discovered purpose in life!

EXAMPLES OF LIFE PURPOSE STATEMENTS

Following are some examples of life purpose statements:

Bob Buford (Business leader)
My life mission is: to transform the latent energy in American Christianity into active energy.[3]

Freya Ottem Hansen (attorney)

To offer compassionate, complete and competent services in law practice; to write words that provoke changes in others, which will please God; and to make of my life one that blesses humanity.[4]

Charlie Wetzel (Writer)

Through writing, teaching and mentoring, I desire to inspire people to greatness by helping them to discover their purpose, to develop their relationship with God and to reach their potential.[5]

A.C. Green (Former NBA Star)

To help young people build self-esteem and character, and learn moral and ethical principles which will help them make responsible decisions.[6]

Your Name:

_____

Your life purpose statement:

_____
_____
_____
_____

ENCOUNTER WITH PURPOSE

PART 8

LIVING OUT
YOUR
LIFE PURPOSE

"Once we have discovered who we are (our design), the next step is to take that information and use it to determine what we can do or what God has designed us to do..."[1]

— Aubrey Malphurs

LIVING OUT YOUR LIFE PURPOSE

Purpose is one of the most important things in your life. Once discovered you will not be the same again! The discovery is just the beginning of this exciting adventure. Once discovered, humans have the greatest possibility to develop their maximum potential. The discovery of your purpose precedes your greatest personal growth and achievements.

At this time, you may have found your purpose, and now you're wondering "Where do I go from here?"I am confident that the information and exercises presented in the previous chapters have helped you see life and yourself from a higher perspective, to connect with yourself on a deeper level, and have stirred or satisfied your pursuit.

> *The discovery of your life purpose precedes your greatest personal growth and greatest achievements!*

After you discover your life purpose, then what? Purpose will require your attention and dedication. Your life purpose may be somewhat new to you, and you will start to lay a foundation to build upon. It will require preparation.

This section focuses on some keys that will help you live your life on purpose today.

CHAPTER 36

PLAN YOUR TRANSITION

It is a good idea to design a strategy to transition into your life purpose.

It is possible that you will want to dedicate yourself completely to your life purpose, after you discover it. What do you do? Do you quit your current job to pursue it? For most people this is not possible for financial reasons. Recognize that you may have just entered into a transitional period in your life. Transitions need to be handled wisely. When you transition, you are no longer here, but you are not yet there! We may become somewhat vulnerable during these times. It is important to make proper decisions that won't sabotage or prolong the transitional process. Consider the meaning of the word transition:

> A passage from one state, stage, subject, or place to another; a movement, development, or evolution, from one form, stage or style to another.[1]

The transition period varies for each one of us and it is determined largely by our pursuit. As with most individuals, you may not have the ability to dedicate twelve hours of your day in the equipping and developing in the area of your purpose. However, your passion will lead you to adjust your schedule to make time for it. Twelve hours may be impossible, but one hour or thirty minutes is not. You may feel as if you are required to put on the brakes because the energy and excitement that has been released is very powerful. If you have to restrain that surge inside you, do it carefully so that you don't stifle or discourage that passion. It is possible for individuals to get frustrated because due to personal and family obligations they may not be able dedicate themselves fully to their newly discovered or confirmed purpose. Bear in mind that you are developing and changing from one stage of your life into another.

Bear in mind that you are developing and changing from one stage of your life into another.

Before David was the king of Israel, he was a shepherd. When Samuel anointed him as the king, David entered into that transition mode. He continued being a shepherd, but he wasn't a shepherd any longer; now he was a king, but he wasn't a king yet. He started "declining" as a shepherd and "ascending" as a king. His transition period took many years. During this period, he wasn't here, but he wasn't there. Yet, one day he was able to say, "I am *here*; I am no longer *there*."

CHAPTER 37

SEEK MENTORS

A mentor is a person of trust that provides counsel and guidance — an indispensable person in our lives.

Mentors transfer wisdom to us through relationship. They teach us out of their experiences, which they gain mostly by their mistakes and discoveries. A mentee is one who is mentored. Through mentorship, a mentee may achieve something in half the time it took the mentor — this is the value of such relationship. Fully committed mentors provide spiritual guidance. They never seek to control or manipulate anyone. As the Apostle Paul with young Timothy, they challenge us to discover and use our gifts, and they always do this with dignity and respect. Another word for a mentee is protégé. Protégé is a French word and it means "One who is protected or trained or whose career is furthered by a person of experience, prominence or influence."[1]

A mentor is a key person to guide you during your transitional period. I have been blessed with several mentors in different seasons of my life, who have challenged me to achieve higher personal and spiritual levels. I have also been fortunate to be a mentor and coach for others. Some have achieved many goals that they set for themselves and others have made major personal changes. On my website, *www.nestorlima.com/praise* you can read some of their testimonies.

> *Without humility, mentorship is impossible.*

Unfortunately, there is a shortage of mentors. The following are a few suggestions to develop good relationships with mentors.

RECOGNIZE THE RELATIONSHIP

A relationship with a mentor is different from the relationships we have with other friends. We have peers, teammates, workout buddies, spouses and relatives. Our relationship with them has a very different nature than with our mentors.

To experience the best out of a mentor-mentee relationship, one must distinguish its uniqueness and respect its difference.

DEMONSTRATE HUMILITY

A person full of pride and with a know-it-all attitude is not ready for mentorship. This mind-set doesn't allow the mentee to receive the guidance or the correction needed.

The acknowledgment of a mentor demonstrates your desire to learn. Without humility, mentorship is impossible. In certain occasion, Jesus got ready to wash Peter's feet, but Peter refused. Jesus told Peter that if he didn't permit it, he would have no relationship with him (John 13:6-9).

TAKE THE INITIATIVE

A mentor is a person who has already achieved a level of success in an area that you aspire. They are not looking to impress anyone. They are humble and possess a genuine passion to help others succeed.

Mentors typically don't pursue mentees. Just because you may have a goal to accomplish, it doesn't mean that mentors are going to hunt you down to help you.

EXPRESS YOUR INTEREST

Passion for mentorship is evidenced by our willingness to leave the comfort zone. Elijah was Elisha's mentor. Elisha's interest for mentorship is revealed in II Kings chapter two.

When Elijah asked his mentee to remain in Gilgal because God had sent him as far as Bethel, Elisha responded by saying, "As the Lord lives and as you live, I will not leave you." (II Kings 2:2) It wasn't insubordination or rebellion. Elisha wasn't being nosy about his mentor's business. He was determined to get the most out of the relationship and he was willing to walk "as far" as Bethel.

This same thing happened after they got to Bethel, and God sent Elijah to Jericho, and then to the Jordan. Elisha's discomfort of walking for miles didn't diminish his desire for mentorship. Other people tried to dissuade him about following his mentor but he remained firm in his persuasion.

MAXIMIZE YOUR TIME

Mentoring opportunities have the potential to save you thousands of dollars and countless headaches.

As Elijah and Elisha went down to the Jordan River, Elijah took out his mantle, folded it and struck the waters. The waters were divided and they crossed the river. Elisha looked attentively as Elijah folded his mantle. How many times did he fold it? How far off the riverbank was he when he folded the mantle? Did he strike the water at an angle? How many times did he strike it? Did he dip his hand in the water?

After they crossed the Jordan River, Elijah looked over his shoulders and asked Elisha what he could do for him before he was taken away. Elisha asked for a double portion of Elijah's spirit to be upon him (II Kings 2:9). Elijah said to Elisha that he would grant the request under one condition: He had to see Elijah when he was taken up.

Elisha was in it to win it! He followed Elijah every step of the way. They were conversing all this time and I imagine that the mentor was doing most of the talking. Suddenly a chariot appeared which separated the two and a whirlwind took Elijah to heaven. While Elisha witnessed this amazing sight, Elijah's mantle fell upon him. He took the mantle, went down to the Jordan River, and did just as his mentor had done before. The waters were divided and he crossed over (II Kings 2:14).

To maximize your time with a mentor you may become their chauffeur for a trip or take them out to lunch. It will require that you leave the comfort zone and invest time, energy and money. Whenever you meet with your mentor, ask questions. Mentors hold valuable information, and the tool for extracting it is questions. Before meeting with your mentor, make a list of the things you would like to ask and be ready to take notes. When I have met with some people who want to be coached or mentored in something in particular, in addition to a notebook, some of them bring a digital recorder. They are maximizing the moment!

My daughter Gianna loves soccer and has been playing for several years in local associations. The granddaughter of a friend began playing when she was nine and went on to play soccer in college, where she broke many records. Her athletic talents covered all her college expenses. During the summer, I contacted Amanda and asked her if she could mentor Gianna, based on her extensive soccer experience. Kindly, she accepted. We met at a restaurant for over an hour. Gianna came prepared with a series of information extracting tools – twenty great questions for her mentor. The transfer of information and wisdom during that time was phenomenal. This time of mentorship elevated Gianna to a higher level of performance in the field. And I happily paid for lunch that afternoon.

Mentorship usually doesn't happen randomly. Pursue it. Schedule it. Expand your knowledge and maximize your opportunities through mentor-mentee relationships.

BENEFITS OF A MENTOR

Following are some key benefits of having a mentor:

- Guidance: Counsel during times of uncertainty.
- Growth: Increased possibilities of achievement.
- Humility: Flexibility to embrace new ideas and methods.
- Direction: Costly mistakes can be avoided.
- Productivity: Achieve more in less time.

In addition to mentorship through relationships, one can also be mentored via books, audio and video recordings.

No one ever achieves something meaningful alone. If you have great goals ahead of you, you will need great people around you. Solicit the expertise and wisdom of those who can deposit knowledge and insight to help you live out your life purpose.

CHAPTER 38

APPRECIATE YOUR
LIFE PURPOSE

Make note of the paradigm shifts you experience from the time you started pursuing purpose, when you discovered it, and beyond.

Something most people experience after discovering their purpose is an accelerated rate of personal growth. It seems to come natural without you working too hard. Don't be too alarmed if you sense your personal growth developing much faster when compared to the past. Documenting your experiences will help you better assess how far you have come.

Deliberately choose to grow in your purpose. I love the following story from *Chicken Soup for the Soul:*

> Two seeds lay side by side in the fertile spring soil. The first seed said, "I want to grow! I want to send my roots deep into the soil beneath me and thrust my sprouts through the earth's crest above

me … I want to unfurl my tender buds like banners to announce the arrival of spring … I want to feel the warmth of the sun on my face and the blessing of the morning dew on my petals!" And so she grew.

The second seed said, "I am afraid. If I send my roots into the ground below, I don't know what I will encounter in the dark. If I push my way through the hard soil above me I may damage my delicate sprouts … what if I let my buds open and a snail tries to eat them? And if I were to open my blossoms, a small child may pull me from the ground. No, it is much better for me to wait until it is safe." And so she waited.

A yard hen scratching around in the early spring ground for food found the waiting seed and promptly ate it.[1]

The moral of this story is that those who are unwilling to risk and grow are swallowed up by life.

What *risks* do you need to take? Have you ever been paralyzed by fear in the past? Extend, develop, multiply, grow … don't fear, you are a success!

RESPECT AND APPRECIATION

You are unique. There is, and there will always be, only one of you! Respectfully embrace your purpose and develop great appreciation for it. You have been designed and equipped for it.

Your respect and appreciation for your life's purpose will increase as you grow and become better equipped to exercise it. You will need this appreciation, especially when you go through valleys in life. There will be moments that

> *Appreciation for your life purpose will help you maintain the focus during challenging times.*

that you will be extremely excited about your purpose and at other times you will question it. Appreciation for your life purpose will help you maintain the focus during challenging times.

You can show respect and appreciation for your purpose in various ways. Accepting, embracing, and fully committing to live out your life purpose, indicates your level of respect and appreciation for it.

CHAPTER 39

RESEARCH CONTINUALLY

Research, research, research!

Continually investigate the area or areas of your purpose. It is great when you read about others whose purpose is similar to yours, and their experiences help reinforce yours.

Reading books is a great way to expand and grow. Many books I have read have either left a lasting impression, or caused a paradigm shift. I enjoy reading books on the topics of leadership, personal development, and human potential.

I encourage you to grow in your purpose. By stepping out of your comfort zone, you may tap into some interesting activities that will align perfectly with your purpose. You will be better equipped to help others, while your growth in your purpose matures as well.

Before discovering my purpose, I didn't know about life coaching. I had only heard the term two or three times. Somehow, I was naturally drawn to it and started doing research. To my surprise, I discovered that this practice has developed in the last twenty years. World-wide it has increased dramatically in the last ten years. Soon after, I was enrolled with the International Coach Academy (ICA) pursuing my Certified Professional Coach designation.

As a Christian life coach, I believe that people are naturally creative and resourceful. I assist them in achieving an array of different goals using a variety of tools. I found that coaching aligns so well with my life purpose. Through coaching and mentoring, I can add value to others and assist them in unlocking God's greatness that is already inside them. As a result, life-purpose coaching is one niche in which I am rapidly developing.

CHAPTER 40

LIVE OUT YOUR LIFE
PURPOSE DAILY

Living out your purpose is a journey, not a destination.

Many people confuse goals with purpose. A goal is the comple-
tion of something you have committed yourself to. For instance, if
you set your mind to lose ten pounds and you did it, your goal is
complete and exists no longer. Goals normally have deadlines.
Purpose is beyond this earth, however! Never see purpose as a
destination but rather as an exciting journey.

One of my daughters wrote a note to her teacher asking her if she
knew her life purpose. The teacher replied to her saying that her
purpose was to become a better teacher. She came home and shared it
with me and she said, "Daddy, this is not her purpose; this is a goal
she has, but I didn't tell her that because I thought it might be disres-
pectful!"

During a brief conversation with our server at a restaurant, I asked him about his purpose. He answered by saying that his purpose, at that moment, was to finish college. When we left the restaurant, my older daughter Gianna who was seven at the time said, "Daddy that is not his purpose. That is a goal!"

You don't have to wait to start living it out. Purpose is not a destination—it's a glorious journey!

The excitement of knowing our purpose causes us to share it with others, not just for the sake of sharing it, but because we want to add value to them. As you share it with others, you become more confident, you see people's reactions and you learn from them. Often they will ask questions that will cause you to grow deeper in your own purpose.

> *Purpose is not a destination—it's a glorious journey!*

Think about small steps that you can take to start living out your purpose on a daily basis. In *The Power of Focus*, the authors note:

> Living your true purpose at the highest level of being indicates that you want to make a difference. It is the most fulfilling place you can be, and offers magnificent rewards. Your life will be joyful. You will have peace of mind and you will be expressing your God-given talents in the most meaningful way possible.[1]

After discovering my purpose, this topic became my dominant thought and center of conversation. I discovered that as I shared about it with people I learned more and I understood it better. Therefore, I kept doing that virtually every day. This book is *one* of the fruits of accepting and determining to live out my purpose on a daily basis!

T. Harv Eker, a great motivational speaker and entrepreneur, teaches that, "Where attention goes, energy flows and results show."[2] One of Eker's mottos is, "What you focus on expands!"[2]

If you focus on sadness, you will find many reasons to be sad and depressed. The feelings become stronger and in one minute, a minor incident is magnified ten thousand times.

As your purpose becomes your focus, you will literally see it grow before your eyes. Your passion and persuasion will grow so strong that nothing or no one will be able to dissuade you!

Since the moment I discovered my purpose, I have made it a goal to motivate or inspire at least one person daily. I can do that at the grocery store, on the basketball court, when I call a credit card company, and even when I receive telemarketer's calls. I take advantage of those opportunities, always being respectful of people's time and responsibilities. I tell them about my daily goal to inspire or motivate at least one person, and then I ask them if they

Living with purpose is the highest and most satisfying way to live.

would like to be that person! The reactions have been interesting. I have never been turned down. I understand that a few kind and motivational words can mean a great deal to someone. One lady asked me, "Do you do this just to do it?" I replied, "I love to invest in people's lives. This is what I live for!" She may have thought I was from a different planet … perhaps I am!

Living with purpose is the highest and most satisfying way to live. Personally, I had never before faced each day of my life with the level of personal confidence, happiness and satisfaction as I do now that I know my life purpose.

Each day is an opportunity for me to continue my development and to make a positive contribution in someone's life. My highest reward is to witness the transformation of people when I have assisted them in discovering their life purpose and to unlock God's greatness inside them. The feelings are indescribable! Few pleasures in life compare!

A life lived on purpose can be summarized as a life of meaning, fulfillment, satisfaction, fullness, and great rewards—a life that is the greatest expression of God's glory on earth!

> *Welcome to the lifestyle of meaning and significance!*

Welcome to the lifestyle of meaning and significance! You have discovered this great treasure. Start enjoying all of its magnificent benefits *today!*

NOTES

Part 1 — Why Pursue Purpose
1. http://www.goodreads.com/quotes/show/144907

Chapter 1 — Your Purpose is The Greatest Expression of God's Glory
1. http://www.merriam-webster.com/dictionary/crown

Chapter 2 — Your Purpose Provides Personal Fulfillment
1. Robert Morris, *From Dream to Destiny,* (Regal Books, Ventura California, 2005), p. 187
2. Aubrey Malphurs, *Planting Growing Churches for the 21st Century,* (Baker Books, Grand Rapids, MI, 2008), p. 79
3. http://www.wisdomquotes.com/cat_purpose.html
4. Napoleon Hill, *Think and Grow Rich,* (Penguin Group Inc, 2003), p. 179
5. DeWayne Owens, *How To Get Rich On Purpose,* (N-H Harmony Publishing, 2002), pp. 38,39,45
6. Jack Canfield, Marc Vincent Hansen and Les Hewitt, *The Power of Focus,* (Health Communications, Inc, 2000), p. 272.

Chapter 3 — Your Purpose is Your Compass
1. T.D. Jakes, *Reposition Yourself,* (ISPN Publishing, 2007), p. 42
2. John C. Maxwell, *Your Road Map For Success,* (Thomas Nelson, 2002), p. 77
3. http://www.merriam-webster.com/dictionary/crown

Chapter 4 — Your Purpose Unlocks Your Success
1. John C. Maxwell, *Your Road Map For Success,* (Thomas Nelson, 2002), p. 12
2. Ibid, p. 11
3. Ibid, p. 30
4. Jack Canfield, Marc Vincent Hansen and Les Hewitt, *The Power of Focus,* (Health Communications, Inc, 2000), p. 288

Chapter 5 — Your Purpose Clarifies Your Past
1. Robert Morris, *From Dream to Destiny,* (Regal Books, Ventura California, 2005), p. 200

Chapter 6 — The Benefits
1. http://www.inspirational-quotes.info – Stan Smith
2. John C. Maxwell, *Developing The Leader Within You,* (Thomas Nelson

Inc, 1992), p. 31

3. Jack Canfield, Marc Vincent Hansen and Les Hewitt, *The Power of Focus*, (Health Communications, Inc, 2000), p. 278.

4. Jimmie L. Lucas Jr., *Custom – Built by God,* (QIM Publishing Company, 2005), p. 57

5. Robert Morris, *From Dream to Destiny,* (Regal Books, Ventura California, 2005), p. 198

Chapter 7— What is Required of You

1. Brazelton, Katherine, *Pathway to Purpose For Women,* (Zondervan, 2005), p. 193

2. Jack Canfield, Marc Vincent Hansen and Les Hewitt, *The Power of Focus*, (Health Communications, Inc, 2000), p. 276

3. http://www.wisdomquotes.com/cat_purpose.html (Felix Adler)

4. Jack Canfield, Marc Vincent Hansen and Les Hewitt, *The Power of Focus*, (Health Communications, Inc, 2000), p. 276

5. Aubrey Malphurs, *Planting Growing Churches for the 21st Century,* (Baker Books, Grand Rapids, MI, 2008), p. 78

Part 3 — Six Dominant Philosophies

1. http://www.wisdomquotes.com/cat_purpose.html (Felix Adler)

2. http://www.knowprose.com/purpose - Excerpt, *The Matrix Reloaded*

3. http://www.pub.umich.edu/daily/1999/sep/09-22-99/edit/edit2.html

4. http://br.answers.yahoo.com/question/index?qid=20070827135003 AAamGZi

5. http://www.seflgrowth.com - by Larry Wayne and Grace Johnston

6. http://www.llewellyn.com (by Carl Llewellyn Weschcke)

7. http://hooponopono.org/pdfs/who-english.pdf - by Ihaleakala Hew Len, Ph.D.

8. http://www.experiencefestival.com/a/Meaning_of_life_-_Popular_beliefs/id/5527140

Chapter 10 — Purpose is Non-Existent

1. http://www.allaboutphilosophy.org/atheism-quotes-faq.htm - Bertrand Russell

2. http://www.iep.utm.edu/nihilism/#H3

3. http://www.cdc.gov/violenceprevention/pdf/Suicide-DataSheet-a.pdfwww.cdc.gov

Chapter 11 — Purpose is Common

1. Aubrey Malphurs, *Planting Growing Churches for the 21st Century*, (Baker Books, Grand Rapids, MI, 2008), p. 79

Chapter 12 — Purpose is Universal
1. http://en.wikibooks.org/wiki/Purpose/3._Looking_For_A_Purpose /What_ Purpose _Can_We_Use%3F

Chapter 13 — Purpose is Chosen
1. http://www.americanhumanist.org/about/manifesto2.php (Humanist Manifesto, II 1973)
2. http://www.youareyourpath.com/index.html
3. Carol Adrienne, *The Purpose Of Your Life*, (Eagle Brook, 1998), pp. 27-28

Chapter 14 — Purpose is Temporal
1. http://friendlyatheist.com/2009/01/03/living-for-the-afterlife

Chapter 15 — Purpose is Assigned
1. Robert Morris, *From Dream to Destiny*, (Regal Books, Ventura California, 2005), p. 186

Part 4 — Misconceptions
1. Art Sepúlveda, *How To Live Life On Purpose*, (Harrison House, Inc., 2004), p. xiv

Chapter 17 — Is Defined by Natural Talents and Gifts
1. Robert Morris, *From Dream to Destiny*, (Regal Books, Ventura California, 2005), p. 193
2. http://www. acgreen.com
3. http://www.acgreen.com/foundation/acletter.html
4. John C. Maxwell, *Your Road Map For Success*, (Thomas Nelson, 2002), pp. 29

Chapter 20 — Meaning and Significance
1. Mary Kay- Ash, *You Can Have It All*, (Prima Publishing, 1995), pp. 92,93
2. Ibid, p. 222

Chapter 21 — Designed on Purpose
1. http://www.merriam-webster.com/dictionary/frame
2. http://www.merriam-webster.com/dictionary/ordain

Chapter 22 — The Anointing and Purpose

1. James Strong, *The New Strong's Complete Dictionary of Bible Words*, (Thomas Nelson Publishing, 1996), p. 442
2. Ibid, p. 443
3. Ibid, p. 504

Chapter 23 — Life's Purpose Definition and Source

1. http://dictionary.reference.com/browse/purpose
2. Victor J. Stenger, *Has Science Found God?* (Prometheus Books, 2005), p. 220
3. John F. Haught, *Science And Religion In Search Of Cosmic Purpose*, (Georgetown University Press, 2000), p. 123
4. Robert Morris, *From Dream to Destiny*, (Regal Books, Ventura California, 2005), p. 186

Chapter 24 — Purpose is Assigned Before Birth

1. Robert Morris, *From Dream to Destiny*, (Regal Books, Ventura California, 2005), p. 193
2. Aubrey Malphurs, *Planting Growing Churches for the 21st Century*, (Baker Books, Grand Rapids, MI, 2008), p. 79

Chapter 25 — Purpose is Both Temporal and Eternal

1. http://en.wikipedia.org/wiki/Ohm
2. http://en.wikipedia.org/wiki/Volt
3. http://en.wikipedia.org/wiki/Ampere
4. http://en.wikipedia.org/wiki/Alzheimer's_disease
5. http://www.newworldencyclopedia.org/entry/Henry_Ford

Section 6 — Seeing The Big Picture

1. Andy Stanley, *Visioneering*, (Multnomah Publishers, 1999), p. 14

Chapter 26 — The Big Picture Revealed

1. Barnes' Notes, Electronic Database, Copyright © 1997, 2003 by Biblesoft, Inc.
2. Jamieson, Fausset, and Brown Commentary, *Electronic Database*. Copyright © 1997, 2003 by Biblesoft, Inc. All rights reserved. Barnes' Notes, Electronic Database, Copyright © 1997, 2003 by Biblesoft, Inc.

Section 7 — Discovering Your Life Purpose

1. Andy Stanley, *Visioneering*, (Multnomah Publishers, 1999), p. 14

Chapter 28 — Have You Really Discovered it?
1. http://www.biographyonline.net/humanitarian/florence-nightingale.html
2. http://www.agnesscott.edu/lriddle/women/nitegale.htm

Chapter 31 — Attitude and Perspective
1. Poem by Rebecca Garcia

Chapter 35 — Write Your Life Purpose Statement
1. Bob Buford, *Halftime*, (Zondervan, 1994), p. 120
2. Ibid, p. 122
3. Ibid, p. 122
4. "Put Your Purpose on Paper," *Discipleship Journal,* issue 71, Sept/Oct 1992, pp. 77-78
5. John C. Maxwell, *Your Road Map For Success,* (Thomas Nelson, 2002), pp. 83
6. http://www.acgreen.com/acgreen/finalsolution.html

Part 8 — Living Out Your Life Purpose
1. Aubrey Malphurs, *Planting Growing Churches for the 21st Century,* (Baker Books, Grand Rapids, MI, 2008), p. 80

Chapter 36 — Plan Your Transition
1. http://www.merriam-webster.com/dictionary/transition

Chapter 37 — Seek Mentors
1. http://www.merriam-webster.com/dictionary/protege

Chapter 38 — Appreciate Your Life Purpose
1. Jack Canfield and Mark Victor Hansen, *Chicken Soup for the Soul,* (Health Communications, Inc. 1993), pp. 220-221

Chapter 40 — Live Out Your Life Purpose Daily
1. Jack Canfield and Mark Victor Hansen, *Chicken Soup for the Soul,* (Health Communications, Inc. 1993), p. 289
2. T. Harv Eker, *Secrets of the Millionaire Mind,* (HarperCollins Publishers, Inc. 2005), p. 143

ENCOUNTER PURPOSE With
Conference

Experience a full day or a weekend immersed in a journey to discover your life purpose.

Expect to achieve the following in this conference:
- Receive inspiration and direction
- Clarify and pursue your life purpose
- Identify your life purpose philosophy
- Correct life purpose misconceptions
- Be coached to discover or reaffirm your life purpose

Speaking invitations
For invitations, or to schedule a conference, please contact Nestor Lima at 817-601-5653 or email Nestor@NestorLima.com.

Have you discovered your purpose?
If you have discovered your life purpose as you read this book, please share it with us. Send your testimonial along with your statement of purpose to Encounter@NestorLima.com.

Encounter 1K
I have an annual goal of assisting at least 1,000 people discover their life purpose. Help me in this effort by becoming part of Encounter1K. Email me at Encounter1K@NestorLima.com for additional information.

NESTOR LIMA
.COM

Life Coaching

Life Coaching works because it helps you release the greatness that resides inside you.

Life Coaching helps you to:
- Acquire a greater degree of self-awareness
- Identify the barriers that keep you from making progress
- Conquer invisible enemies
- Overcome spiritual and personal obstacles
- Enhance your natural gifts
- Clarify your life purpose
- Complete unfinished goals
- Awaken dying passions
- Revive buried dreams

If you are ready to maximize your life, I offer a complimentary 15-minute coaching session. Schedule your session by visiting my website www.NestorLima.com.

NESTOR LIMA MINISTRIES
P.O. Box 2007
Hurst, Texas 76053
www.NestorLima.com
Nestor@NestorLima.com
Tel. 817-601-5653

Life Coaching Testimonials

Often people achieve their goals with the assistance of a Life Coach. Following are some of the experiences of several of my clients:

"What I got from coach Lima in a word is direction. This is the first time in the last four years that I felt that I have control over my future. I have a new sense of direction compatible with whom I was created to be! I have never met or heard of someone that can so effectively coach and empower you on a personal basis to find your purpose like coach Lima. You will produce the most when you're living a life of purpose."

Karen Chaparro, Co-owner, Gmaids.com

"Coaching helped me transition to a newly discovered level of achievement and self-realization. It birthed an appreciation for myself and all I am capable of. With the wisdom of my Coach I was able to unfold and develop my character ... It has taken my schema of life and self-concept to a higher level!"

Rebecca Garcia

"Nestor created a very safe place to talk ... He was able to help me take a step back and really understand where I was stuck. I was able to attack my objectives head on with some of the theories Nestor introduced to me...I found myself growing by the week. His coaching techniques are useful in everyday and business life. Nestor also was right there with me when I wanted to find my spirituality again and needed some guidance on how to handle such a powerful awakening. Anyone looking to grow as an individual should seriously consider coaching from Nestor Lima."

Candy Myura, Executive Coach

"You literally held my hand and took me to the place where I always wanted to be. Your coaching has been a process of self-discovery. I can't thank you enough for helping me become my own leader! I don't let the thoughts control me; I control them now ... this was the biggest barrier in moving forward."

Anshu Patanjali, Life Coach/Trainer

6957731R0

Made in the USA
Charleston, SC
03 January 2011